# 外国人学中国语
# 1

## CHINESE LANGUAGE LEARNING
## FOR FOREIGNERS

顾问　张志公

主编　王福祥

副主编　杨天戈　周奎杰

责任编委　李宪生　黄友义　刘宁　贾寅淮

华语教学出版社　北京
SINOLINGUA BEIJING

First Edition    1993
Sixth Printing    2006

ISBN 7 - 80052 - 309 - 8
Copyright 1993 by Sinolingua
Published by Sinolingua
24 Baiwanzhuang Road, Beijing 100037, China
Tel: (86) 10-68995871
Fax: (86) 10-68326333
http//: www. sinolingua.com.cn
E-mail: hyjx@ sinolingua.com.cn
Printed by Beijing Foreign Languages Printing House
Distributed by China International
Book Trading Corporation
35 Chegongzhuang Xilu, P.O. Box 399
Beijing 100044, China

*Printed in the People's Republic of China*

# 说　明

一、本教材共 13 单元,计 40 课。第 1 单元为语音阶段,计 4 课;2—13 单元为正课文,每 1 单元各 3 课,每课由课文、生词、课文注释、句型和练习五项内容组成,其中"练习"部分量较大,旨在通过较多练习,达到言语训练的目的。

二、每课生词安排按名词、代词、形容词、动词、数词、量词、副词、介词、连词、叹词、助词、地名专词、短语、固定词组顺序排列。全书共有生词 1578 个(内含专有名词、地名 55 个),共中 H.S.K 所列甲级词汇 672 个,乙级词汇 313 个,丙级词汇 102 个,三类等级词占全部生词的 72.6%。每单元中的补充生词,不要求都能掌握和运用。

三、每单元的小结,除第 1 单元为语音小结外,其他各单元小结都在本单元所学内容基础上加以扩展,包括常用交际用语、语法简说、了解中国、趣味汉语、汉字常识等项栏目,对于课文内容既有归纳总结,又有引申和发挥,以达到巩固技能与知识的目地。

四、本教材所用语法中的句子成分符号是:——主语、＝谓、～～～宾语、< 　 > 补语、( 　 )定语、〔 　 〕状语、～～～兼语。

# Guide to the Use of the Book

1. This teaching material is in 13 units covering a total of 40 lessons. Unit One focuses on pronunciation and includes four lessons. Unit Two to Thirteen include regular texts with three lessons to each unit. Each lesson consists of text, vocabulary, explanatory notes, sentence patterns and exercises. Of these , the major item is "Exercises", the aim being to give language training through plenty of drills.

2. The vocabulary of each lesson is arranged according to the following order: noun, pronoun, adjective, verb, numeral, measure word, adverb, preposition, conjunction, exclamation, auxiliary word, place name and proper noun, short phrase, and fixed word group. The book presents 1,578 new words (including 55 proper nouns and place names), of which 672 are A-level words listed by H.S.K. or Chinese Language Level Test Programme (underlined with ══ ), 313 are B-level words (underlined with ___ ), 102 are C-level words (underlined with ∼∼∼). Together, they account for 72.6 percent of the total number of new words in the book. The students are not required to memorize and use all the supplementary new words in each unit.

3. Except for the pronunciation summary in Unit One, all other unit summaries are developed on the basis of the material taught in the respective units. They include such items as "Communicative Expression", "A Brief Introduction to Grammar", "Understanding China", "Humour" and "Introduction to Chinese Characters". These items not only summarize the content of the texts; they also extend and elaborate on them so as to consolidate the students' skill and knowledge.

4. The symbols standing for the different parts of speech used in the grammar system of this book are: ___ for subject, ══ for predicate, ∼∼∼ for object, ‹ › for complement, ( ) for attribute, [ ] for adverbial, ∼∼∼ for object-subject.

# 前　言

　　这套教材的总名称叫《外国人学中国语》。这是根据同一底本分别编出的包括英、俄、日、德、法、西、阿拉伯、韩文等八种不同文本的系列教材,供不同国家和地区的人在学习中国语的起始阶段(零起点)时使用。

　　据我们的经验,不同国家和地区的人学习中国语,除了会碰到一些共同的问题和困难外,更多的是会碰到一些各自不同的问题和困难,因此应当深入总结学习中国语的一些特殊的规律,分别制定出适应某些特定国家和地区的人的教学法,包括编写出有针对性的教材。我们目前的工作,就是把这种设想付诸实践的第一步。

　　这套教材,除了分别用不同语言对课文进行翻译、加以注解和说明外,还着重从语音系统、语法体系、交际习惯和国情文化背景四个方面对中国语和学习者的母语进行比较,使他们不仅能正确理解和接受那些对比反差极大的规律和习惯,而且还能区别和掌握那些反差较小但又绝对不可忽略、混淆的细微之处。这是所有学习第二语言的人都必须掌握的方法、都应当争取达到的目标。我们这套教材,希望为各国的中国语学习者在实现这个目标方面提供有效的帮助,使他们更快地实现两种语言之间的沟通和过渡。

　　从教学法体系来讲,本套教材采取的是突出交际法原则的一种综合教学法。交际法原则近年来在语言教学(主要是外语教学)中使用很广,并取得显著成效。但在对外汉语教学中使用的历史不长,很值得进一步试验和推广。汉语作为非形态语,尤其适合交际法的推广和应用。汉语基本上没有形态变化,因此在汉语学习的初级阶段,在无须借助于复杂句型就可进行简单交际的阶段,交际法的运用应该具有比在形态语中更为方便有利之处。这是我们选用交际法为本教材所遵循的基本法则的原因。教材中每篇课文围绕一定的话题领域,在特定的情景中展开交际,通过交际进行言语训练,并将相关的功能、意念项目编织其中。但任何事情都不能绝对化,交际法本身也存在一定的局限性。因此我们在编写教材时,并不处处固守交际法的樊篱。为了更合理地兼顾言语训练和语言系统的学习这两方面的需要,我们对语音知识、语法知识作了相对集中而又简明扼要的安排处理,而不使之流于过分支离破碎。并吸取结构法的优点,安排了一定数量的句型练习。这种集众家之所长,而不死守一家路数的作法,并非我们的发明创造,而是较多同行共有的经验。至于我们作得是否成功、结合得是否协调、自然,将有待于实践的检验。

　　汉字是汉语学习过程中的一只拦路虎。许多外国人觉得汉语难学,很重要的原因在于汉字难于掌握。在交际法教学的初级阶段,如果一开始就把汉字这个包袱背起来,要求交际能力的培养与汉字的识记同步,必然使初学者望而却步。因此我们这本教材分作两册,第一册只借拼音作拐棍,以拼音带口语,进行交际训练。但每一单元之末尾安排了一栏〈汉字常识〉,以通俗生动的例子,向学生讲述有关汉字的故事,使他们初步了解汉字的构造法(六书的简单原则),熟悉汉字的笔划结构,并初步认识少量汉字。从第二册起,课文中汉字开始和拼音结合,学生除继续培养交际能力外,增加了识记和书写汉字的任务。这是一种语言和文字逐步合流的办法。这样作,可以在起始阶段绕开汉字,但又不会造成后面汉字突然大量出现,难点过于集中的那样一种毛病。

这套教材开始注意到语言教学过程中的文化背景知识导入问题。并力求改变汉语教材过于呆板的面貌,增加了教材的趣味性。教材增加了插图,使图文结合,并力争做 到图文并茂,在编排方面也做了较大改进。

这套教材是在世界汉语教学学会顾问张志公先生指导下,以北京外国语学院的汉语和外语教师为基干力量,集体编写出来的。张志公先生最先提出了这套教材的指导原则和总体设计。编写过程中,听取了专家、同行们的建议和意见,并参照中国国家汉办颁布的汉语水平测试大纲,认真进行了修改。在北京外国语学院工作的部分专家参加了审稿。华语教学出版社的领导、编辑始终与我们亲密合作,为教材的编写、出版作出了可贵的努力。尤其是整个计划一开始就得到国家汉办的关切和强有力的支持。可以说,我们是踏着同行为我们铺垫出来的路基前进,是在诸多方面力量的支撑、帮助下进行工作的。离开上述条件,我们难以有所成就。这套教材如能在我们所设想的方面取得某些预期的效果、在某些方面比之已有教材能有所改进的话,我们不能不强调我们的支持者与合作者的作用。但由于水平所限,这套教材定会有一些疏漏与不足,我们欢迎来自各方面的批评和指正。

杨天戈

1993 年 7 月

# Introduction

This set of teaching material, titled *Chinese Language Learning for Foreigners*, is based on an original meta-text. This set, comprising eight different versions: English, Russian, Japanese, German, French, Spanish, Arabic and Korean, is designed for use by beginners of Chinese in a wide range of countries and regions.

According to our experience, though learners of Chinese from different countries and regions share certain common problems and difficulties, more often they are apt to encounter their own distinctive problems and difficulties. We therefore comprehensively sum up some special points governing Chinese language learning so as to respectively formulate various pedagogics to suit the needs of people of different countries and regions and compile special textbooks for people of different cultures. Our present effort is to put this concept into practice.

This set of teaching material, apart from translating, annotating and explaining the texts in the different languages, tries also to compare and contrast the Chinese language with the learners' native language in terms of phonetic system, grammar structure, communicative conventions and national and cultural background. Learners are helped not only to correctly understand and accept the rules and conventions that contrast sharply with those in their native language; they are also helped to differentiate and master those more subtle points which do not contrast sharply but must never be neglected or confused. Presented here are methods that we feel anyone who learns a second language must master; they are a goal hopefully to be achieved. We trust that this set of teaching material can provide learners in various countries with effective assistance to reach this goal, so that they can move across from one language to another smoothly and quickly.

As for pedagogical system, this set of teaching material has adopted a comprehensive type of pedagogics with emphasis on communicative principles. The communicative approach has been used very extensively in language teaching (mainly in foreign language teaching for Chinese learners) in recent years with notable success. But as it is fairly new in the teaching of Chinese as a foreign language, it is worthwhile to further experiment and promote its application. As a non-inflexional language, Chinese is particularly suitable for the popularization and application of the communicative approach. At the preliminary stage where beginners may be able to converse without using complex sentence patterns, it is more convenient to use the communicative approach in teaching Chinese than in inflexional languages. We have therefore adopted the communicative approach mainly in writing this book. Each text centres around a topic; communication is in the context of a given background; language training is realized through communication; relevant functions and conceptual items are woven into the communications. However, nothing can be considered as absolute. The communicative approach by itself has certain limitations and so the book is not confined within the limits of the communicative approach. In an attempt to facilitate both language training and study of the linguistic system, brief introduction to pronunciation and grammar are grouped together so as to avoid fragmentary presentation. At the same time, the advantages of the structural approach are recognized and incorporated in the work, and some pattern drills are included.

This approach of incorporating the benefits of different methods without confining the work within the limits of any one method is not our invention. It is in fact an approach shared by many language teachers. As to whether our efforts will be successful and the integration be coordinated and natural, only time and practice will tell.

One obstacle in learning Chinese is its writing system. Many foreigners find it difficult to learn Chinese largely because they have difficulty memorizing the written characters. If, at the preliminary stage of the communicative system of instruction, we take on the characters and ask the learners to train their communicative competence while memorizing the Chinese characters, we would undoubtedly intimidate our beginners. We have therefore divided the material into two separate books. Book I uses romanization only to facilitate oral practice and carry out communicative training. However, at the end of each unit there is an 'Introduction to Chinese Characters' in which simple and interesting stories about Chinese characters are told. The students are enabled to initially understand the way Chinese characters are formed (the principles of the six categories of Chinese characters), familiarize themselves with the strokes and structures of the characters and commit a small number of them to memory. Starting from Book II, Chinese characters are added, combined with romanization. Apart from improving their communicative competence, the students must also learn to read and write Chinese characters. In this way, the oral and written aspects of the language are gradually integrated. This allows getting acquainted with written characters at the preliminary stage while avoiding having to deal with a large number of difficult written characters showing up all of a sudden at a later stage.

This material takes into consideration the introduction of cultural background in language teaching, aiming to discard a prevailing rigid style found in textbooks for teaching Chinese as a foreign language; it is designed to be more interesting. Included are many pictures and drawings.

This set of teaching material is compiled with the collective effort of teachers of Chinese and foreign languages from Beijing Foreign Studies University under the guidance of Mr Zhang Zhigong, consultant of World Chinese Language Teaching Society, who initiated the basic principles and general layout of the book. While writing the book we referred to the opinions and suggestions raised by experts and colleagues and the Chinese Language Level Testing Programme issued by China's National Office of Chinese Language Teaching. Some foreign experts working at Beijing Foreign Studies University went over the manuscripts. Betty Chandler, with Foreign Languages Press, China, contributed her language skills to the English part of this book. The leaders and editors of Sinolingua, the publisher of this set of material, have all along cooperated closely with us and have made a valuable contribution to the compiling and publishing of the book.

Moreover, the National Office of Chinese Language Teaching has, from the very outset, shown concern and strong support for the project. We must acknowledge that we have been guided by the footsteps of other language teachers, and that we have worked with the support and help given us by various institutes.

If the book succeeds as we hope and proves in certain aspects to be an improvement on exising textbooks, the efforts of those who supported and cooperated with us must be emphasized. Criticisms and corrections of the material are most welcome.

*Yang Tiange*
July 1993

# CONTENTS

# Lesson One

nǐ  you

n-i nǐ

wǒ  I(me)

w-o wǒ

tā  he, she, it (him, her, it)

t-a tā

nǐmen  you (plural)
e-n en
m-en men

wǒmen  we (us)
e-n en
m-en men

tāmen  they(them)
e-n en
m-en men

Huānyíng nǐ!  Welcome!
a—n an    i—ng ing
u—an uan  y—ing yíng
h—uan huān

Xièxie!  Thanks!
i—e ie
x—ie xiè

1

# Vocabulary

| | | | | | |
|---|---|---|---|---|---|
| nǐ | *pro.* | you (singular) | wǒmen | *pro.* | we(us) |
| wǒ | *pro.* | I (me) | tāmen | *pro.* | they (them) |
| tā | *pro.* | he, she, it（him, her,it) | huānyíng | *v.* | welcome |
| | | | xièxie | *v.* | thank |
| nǐmen | *pro.* | you (plural) | | | |

# Pronunciation

## 1. Initials

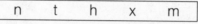

n    t    h    x    m

Initials are consonants placed at the beginning of each syllable.

 **n**  The tip of the tongue touches the upper gum; the vocal cords vibrate; and air is let out through the nasal cavity.

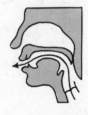 **t**  The tip of the tongue touches the upper gum; the vocal cords do not vibrate; and a puff of air explodes through the obstruction.

 **h**  The root of the tongue is raised close to the soft palate; the vocal cords do not vibrate; and air is let out with friction between the root of the tongue and the soft palate.

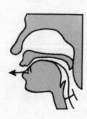 **x**  The tongue blade is raised close to the hard palate; the vocal cords do not vibrate; and air is let out with friction between the tongue blade and the hard palate.

 m   The lips are closed; the vocal cords vibrate; and air is let out through the nasal cavity.

## 2. Finals

Finals are vowels placed after initials or phoneme groups centering around vowels. There are simple, compound, and nasal vowels.

Simple vowels

A simple vowel is a final composed of a single vowel sound.

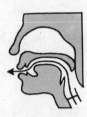 i   The mouth cavity is narrowed; the tongue is placed naturally in a flat position close to the upper gum without causing any obstruction; the vocal cords vibrate.

 a   The mouth is opened wide; the tongue is placed naturally farthest from the upper gum without being very close to either the front or the rear; the vocal cords vibrate.

Compound vowels

Finals made up of two or more vowels are called compound vowels.

    i-e   ie

Nasal vowels   en   uan   ing

Finals ending with nasal consonants are called nasal vowels.

    e-n   en

    a-n   an   u-an   uan

    i-ng   ing   (In articulating ng the root of the tongue is raised against the soft palate; the vocal cords vibrate; and air is let out through the nasal cavity. )

A few syllables do not add consonants. For example:

w-o   wo
y-ing   ying

## 3. W and Y

W is pronounced as u; y is pronounced as i. W and y are substitutes for u and i. They are used in order to make the syllables stand out. Further explanations will be given under the rules of spelling.

## 4. Tones

A tonal language, Chinese has four tones which help differentiate meanings. Tone signs are indicated above the vowel in all cases.

The first tone is a high flat tone. During articulation the tone remains high and flat, e.g. tā. The tone mark is written as ¯.

The second tone is a rising tone. During articulation the tone rises from semi-high pitch to the highest pitch, e.g. yíng. The tone mark is written as ´.

The third tone is a winding tone. The tone starts from low pitch and descends then rises to a high pitch, e.g. nǐ. The tone mark is written as ˇ .

The fourth tone is a falling tone. During articulation the tone starts from the highest pitch and goes down close to the lowest pitch, e.g. xiè. The tone mark is written as ˋ.

If we place the tones on a five-level scale, the four tones will look like this:

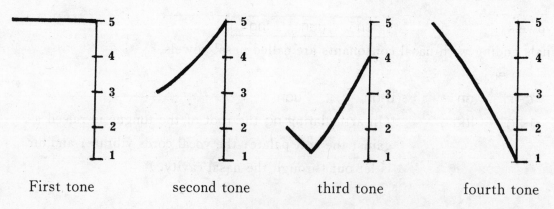

First tone          second tone          third tone          fourth tone

5. How does Chinese compare with English in pronunciation?

n   This initial is equivalent to the [n] in *nice* and *not*.

t   This initial is equivalent to the [t] in *tea* and *time*.

h   Its near equivalent in English is [h], but the h in Chinese is pronounced with a stronger friction as air is exhaled from between the root of the tongue and the soft palate.

x   There is no English equivalent for x. Native speakers of English often pronounce x as [ʃiː] (she). To pronounce x correctly, the lips should not protrude, while the tongue blade, not the tip, is raised close to the hard palate.

m   The English equivalent of m is [m] as in *mother* and *mile*. M in Chinese is never used to end a syllable.

i   This final is very close to the [iː] sound in *bee* and *teach*.

a   Its equivalent in English is [aː] as in *father* and *palm*; a in Chinese differs from the English [aː] somewhat as the former sounds more like a central than a back vowel.

### Exercises

1. Read aloud the following initials:
   n   t   h   x   m
2. Read aloud th following finals:
   i   a
   ie
   an   en   uan   ing
3. Pronounce the following:
   n-i   t-a   w-o
   y-ing   h-uan   x-ie
4. Tone discrimination:
   ī   í   ǐ   ì      ā   á   ǎ   à

| nī | ní | nǐ | nì | | tā | tá | tǎ | tà |
|----|----|----|----|--|----|----|----|----|
| wō | wó | wǒ | wò | | huān | huán | huǎn | huàn |
| yīng | yíng | yǐng | yìng | | xiē | xié | xiě | xiè |

## 5. Read aloud the following new words:

nǐ　wǒ　tā

nǐmen　wǒmen　tāmen

huānyíng　xièxie

## 6. Look at the pictures and speak Chinese:

## 7. Substitution drills:

Huānyíng
$$\begin{cases} \text{nǐ.} \\ \text{tā.} \\ \text{nǐmen.} \\ \text{tāmen.} \end{cases}$$

Xièxie
$$\begin{cases} \text{nǐ.} \\ \text{tā.} \\ \text{nǐmen.} \\ \text{tāmen.} \end{cases}$$

# Lesson Two

—Nǐ hǎo!   How do you do!
(How are you!)

—Nǐ hǎo!   How do you do!
(How are you!)

  a-o  ao
  h-ao  hǎo

shǒu  hand

o-u  ou
sh-ou  shǒu

wò-shǒu  shake hands

—Duìbuqǐ!  I am sorry!
—Méiguānxi.  That's all right.

u-i  ui  d-ui  duì
b-u  bù
q-i  qǐ
e-i  ei  m-ei  méi
g-u-an  guān
x-i  xì

—Zàijiàn!  Good-bye!
—Zàijiàn!  Good-bye!

a-i  ai  z-ai  zài
j-i-an  jiàn

7

nǚ woman          nán man
n—ü nǚ           n-an nán

## Vocabulary

| | | | | | |
|---|---|---|---|---|---|
| shǒu | *n.* | hand | duìbuqǐ | (I am) sorry |
| nǚ | *n.* | woman | méiguānxi | It's all right. It |
| nán | *n.* | man | | doesn't matter. |
| hǎo | *a.* | good, well | zàijiàn | good-bye |
| wòshǒu | *v.* | shake hands | | |

## Pronunciation

1. Initials

b    The lips are closed to cause obstruction; the vocal cords vibrate; and air in the oral cavity is compressed to pronounce with plosion.

d    The tip of the tongue touches the upper teeth and gum to cause obstruction; the vocal cords do not vibrate; and air is compressed in the oral cavity to pronounce with plosion.

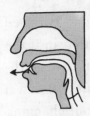
z The tip of the tongue touches the narrow passage between the upper and lower teeth (without sticking it out) to cause obstruction; the vocal cords do not vibrate; the obstruction is quickly removed with some explosion; plosion is then turned into friction, during which air is exhaled gently.

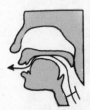
j The tongue blade is raised to press the hard palate so as to cause obstruction; articulation is similar to that for z; the vocal cords do not vibrate; affrication is used (starting with a sort of plosion which changes into friction).

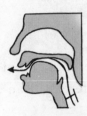
q The position and manner of articulation are the same as for j; the difference lies in the fact that j is unaspirated (the obstruction is removed by using the air in the oral cavity), whereas q is aspirated (the obstruction is removed by a strong puff of air from the lung).

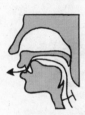
sh The tip of the tongue rolls up to press the hard palate, causing obstruction; the vocal cords do not vibrate; and air is exhaled from between the tip of the tongue and the hard palate.

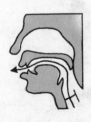
g The root of the tongue is raised to touch the soft palate, causing obstruction; the vocal cords do not vibrate; the obstruction is removed by plosion using the unaspirated method.

## 2. Finals
Simple vowels

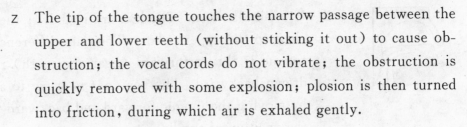

| u  ü |
| --- |

u This vowel can be found in the nasal vowel uɑn introduced in Lesson One. To articulate this vowel the lips should be rounded and protruded; the tongue is raised close to the upper palate, the root of the tongue is drawn near the throat; the vocal cords vibrate.

ü Ü is similar to u. The lips are rounded; the tongue is raised close to the upper palate. The only difference is that in ü the tongue is thrust forward (near the teeth) rather than withdrawn backward. The beginner may try to articulate ü and u by moving the tongue forward and backward without changing the position of the lips.

Compound vowels

| ao | ou | ai | ei | ui |
|---|---|---|---|---|

| a-o | ao | | o-u | ou |
|---|---|---|---|---|
| a-i | ai | | e-i | ei |
| u-i | ui | | | |

Nasal vowels

| an | ian |
|---|---|

| a-n | an | | i-an | ian |
|---|---|---|---|---|

## 3. Tones

One of the main characteristics of Chinese pronunciation is the differentiation of meaning by tones. Characters with the same initials and finals have different meanings if the tones are different. For example:

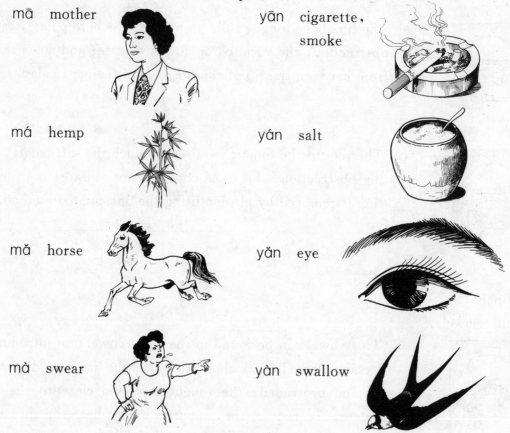

mā mother

má hemp

mǎ horse

mà swear

yān cigarette, smoke

yán salt

yǎn eye

yàn swallow

4. How does Chinese compare with English in pronunciation?

b   [b] in English (as in *bed*) is a near equivalent. The Chinese b is voiceless,
    whereas the English [b] is voiced.

d   [d] in English is a near equivalent (as in *do*). The Chinese d is voiceless,
    whereas the English [d] is voiced.

z   It is close to the combination of [d] and [z] as in *beds* and *friends*.

j   There is no equivalent in English. Native speakers of English often pronounce
    it as [dʒ] (as in *joy*). This error can be corrected by referring to the pronunci-
    ation of x in Chinese. The lips do not protrude, and it is the tongue blade
    rather than the tongue tip that touches the hard palate.

q   There is no equivalent in English. Native speakers of English often pronounce
    q as [tʃ] as in *teach*. Please refer to x and j for correct pronunciation.

sh  Its close equivalent is [ʃ] (as in *she* and *shoe*). But the sh in Chinese is not pro-
    nounced with protruded lips.

g   Its close equivalent is [g] as in *go* and *get*. The g in Chinese is voiceless,
    whereas the English [g] is voiced.

u   Its equivalent is [uː] as in *too* and *who*.

ü   There is no equivalent in English. It is close to the u sound in such French
    words as *lune* and *rue*.

**Exercises**

1. Read aloud the following initials:
     b  d  z  j  q  sh  g

2. Read aloud the following finals:
     u  ü
     ao  ou  ai  ei  ui
     an  ian

3. Pronounce the following:
     h-ao  hǎo          sh-ou  shǒu
     d-ui  duì          m-ei  méi
     g-u-an  guān       z-ai  zài
     j-i-an  jiàn       n-ü  nǚ
     n-an  nán          b-u  bù

4. Tone discrimination:

hāo háo hǎo hào      duī duí duǐ duì

qī qí qǐ qì      mēi méi měi mèi

guān guán guǎn guàn      bū bú bǔ bù

xī xí xǐ xì      tā tá tǎ tà

xiē xié xiě xiè      shōu shóu shǒu shòu

5. Read aloud the following new words:

hǎo    wòshǒu    shǒu

duìbuqǐ    méiguānxi

nán    nǚ    zàijiàn

6. Sustitution drills:

Nǐ
Nǐmen } hǎo.

7. Look at the pictures and speak Chinese:

8. Sound discrimination:

d-t    t-d    d-d    t-t

tǎ-dǎ    dī-tī    duì-tuì    dù-tù    duō-tuō

j-q    j-j    q-q    q-j

jǐ-qǐ    jiàn-qiàn    jiā-qiā    qīn-jīn

nǔ-nǚ    uan-üan    uen-üen

# Lesson Three

—Tā shì shuí?   Who is he?

—Tā shì wǒ de bàba.   He is my father.

—Bàba, tā shì wǒ de péngyou.   Dad, this is a friend of mine.

—Bófù, nín hǎo!   How do you do, Uncle (sir)!

nán rén   man

nǚ rén   woman

lǎo rén   old person

# Vocabulary

| | | | | | | |
|---|---|---|---|---|---|---|
| bàba | *n.* | father | shuí | *pro.* | who |
| péngyou | *n.* | friend | nín | *pro.* | you (respectful form, singular) |
| bófù | *n.* | uncle (father's elder brother, the term often used as a respectful form on the father of one's friend) | lǎo | *a.* | old |
| | | | shì | *v.* | to be |
| | | | de | | (a function word denoting affiliation or modification) |
| rén | *n.* | person, people | | | |

# Pronunciation

1. Initials

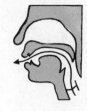

p  P is similar to b. Their position and manner of articulation are the same (the lips are closed to cause obstruction; the vocal cords do not vibrate; the obstruction is removed by plosion). They are different in that b is unaspirated, whereas p is aspirated.

f  The upper teeth are placed on the inside edge of the lower lip to cause obstruction; the vocal cords do not vibrate; and air is exhaled from between the lower lip and teeth with friction.

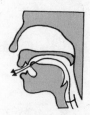

l  The tip of the tongue is raised to touch the upper gum; the vocal cords vibrate; and air is exhaled from both sides of the tongue blade.

r  The tip of the tongue rolls up to touch the hard palate; the vocal cords vibrate; and air is exhaled with friction from between the tip of the tongue and the hard palate.

## 2. Finals
Simple vowels

| e    o |

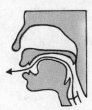

e    The mouth is half open; the tongue is placed in mid position; the lips open naturally; the vocal cords vibrate.

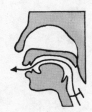

ê    In terms of lip-rounding, ê is basically the same as e. The difference lies in the fact that in ê the tongue is moved forward; the tip of the tongue softly touches the lower teeth; the lip-rounding becomes a bit flat. The beginner may try to articulate ê and e alternately by moving the tongue forward and backward. ê can never stand by itself. It is combined with i and u to form compound vowels. In writing, the ˆ is omitted as for example in ie and ue.

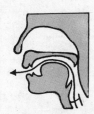

o    In o the tongue position is similar to that in e except that the lips are rounded. Beginners may try to articulate o and e alternately by changing the lip-rounding.

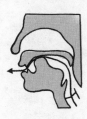

-i    The Chinese alphabet i is not pronounced as i when it is placed after retroflex consonants. -i stands for the vowel sound that goes after the retroflex consonant. For example, in the syllable shi, -i stands for the vowel sound that follows the retroflex consonant sh. It is produced by vibrating the vocal cords, with the tongue rolled up.

Nasal vowels

| in    eng |

i-n    in     e-ng    eng

## 3. Pronunciation

In natural speech there is a soft-toned syllable which must be pronounced softly. The syllable also becomes short, vague and toneless.

There are two ways to read soft-toned syllables: high pitch and low pitch. Examples of high pitch syllables:

nǐmen    wǒmen    tāmen

This syllable is soft and short. It falls on the fourth degree of the five-scale chart:

Examples of low pitch syllables:

    bàba   xièxie

This syllable falls on the second degree of the five-scale chart:

Toneless syllables appear in the following words:

1. The last syllable of certain nouns and pronouns. For example:

    nǐmen   wǒmen   péngyou

2. The second syllable of some reiterative locution. For example:

    bàba   xièxie

3. Some function words. For example:

    wǒ de bàba

In writing, no tone marks appear on toneless syllables.

4. How does Chinese compare with English in pronunciation?

    p     Its equivalent is [p] as in *pen* and *pie*.

    f     Its equivalent is [f] as in *five* and *fine*.

    l     Its equivalent is [l] as in *low* and *look*.

    r     Its near equivalent is [r] as in *red* and *rose*. Unlike the English [r], r in Chinese is not pronounced by first protruding and rounding the lips.

    e     Its near equivalent is [ə] as in *about* and *alive*. But e is pronounced longer in Chinese.

    e     Its equivalent is [e] as in *bed* and *pet*.

    o     Its near equivalent is [ɔ:] as in *four* and *more*.

## Exercises

1. Read aloud the following initials:

    p   f   l   r

16

2. Read aloud the following finals:

    o   e   ê   eng   in

3. Read aloud the following:

    bà   bó   fù   de   shì   shuí

    rén   nín   lǎo   péng   you

4. Tone discrimination:

    shì       shí

              (ten)

    shuí       shuǐ           shuì

             (water)         (sleep)

    nǐmen      wǒmen      tāmen      péngyou

    wǒ de bàba      xièxie      lǎorén

5. Read aloud the following new words:

    bàba   bófù   péngyou

    nánrén   nǚrén   lǎorén

    shuí   shì   nín

6. Substitution drills:

                   bàba.

                   māma (mother).

    Tā shì wǒ de    gēge (elder brother).

                   dìdi (younger brother).

                   péngyou.

7. Spelling exercise (fill in the blanks with i or y):

    j＿＿＿ā,   ＿＿＿ā      j＿＿＿ě,   ＿＿＿ě

    x＿＿＿ào,   ＿＿＿ào      j＿＿＿ān,  ＿＿＿ān,   ＿＿＿ou

8. Sound discrimination:

    bō          pō          bā          pā

    nán        lán        nǎo       lǎo

    fēn        fēng      lín       líng

    lù         lǜ         nǔ        nǚ

bóbo (uncle)    pópo (aunt)

9. Answer the following questions:

Tā shì shuí?

Tā shì wǒ de

# Lesson Four

chá  tea

kāfēi  coffee

sānmíngzhì
sandwich

Zhōngguó cài
Chinese dishes

—Zhè shì shénme?  What's this?
—Zhè shì chá.  It's tea.
Zhè shì Zhōngguó cài.
This is Chinese food.

—Nà shì shénme?  What's that?
—Nà shì kāfēi.  That's coffee.
Nà shì sānmíngzhì.
That's a sandwich.

—Wǒ hē chá.  I am drinking tea.
Wǒ chī Zhōngguó cài.  I am eating Chinese food.

19

# Vocabulary

| | | | | | | |
|---|---|---|---|---|---|---|
| chá | *n.* | tea | zhè | *pro.* | this |
| kāfēi | *n.* | coffee | shénme | | what |
| sānmíngzhì | *n.* | sandwich | nà | *pro.* | that |
| Zhōngguó | *n.* | China | hē | *v.* | drink |
| cài | *n.* | dish | chī | *v.* | eat |

# Pronunciation

1. Initials

zh  The tip of the tongue rolls up to touch the upper gum causing obstruction; the vocal cords do not vibrate; the obstruction is removed by using affrication (plosion followed by friction); it is unaspirated.

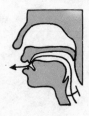

ch  The position and manner of articulation is the same as in zh; only ch is aspirated, whereas zh is not.

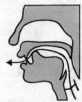

c  The tip of the tongue is laid flat to touch the narrow passage between the upper and lower teeth, causing obstruction; the vocal cords do not vibrate; the obstruction is removed by using affrication; it is aspirated. C can be contrasted to z. C is aspirated while z is not. C can also be contrasted to ch. Ch is a retroflex sound while c is not.

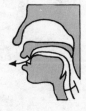

s  The tip of the tongue is laid flat to touch the narrow passage between the upper and lower teeth, causing obstruction; the vocal cords do not vibrate; the air is exhaled with friction from between the narrow passage. S can be contrasted to sh. Sh is a retroflex sound while s is not.

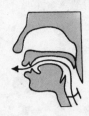

k The root of the tongue is raised to touch the soft palate causing obstruction; the vocal cords do not vibrate; the obstruction is removed by plosion; it is aspirated. K can be contrasted to g. K is aspirated while g is not.

## 2. Finals

Simple vowels

-i

The vowel sound -i in such syllables as zhi, chi, shi and ri are not pronounced as i. -i stands for the vowel sound that follows the retroflex consonants h, ch, sh and r.

Z, c and s can also combine with -i to form syllables zi, ci, and si. Again the -i is not pronounced as i but stands for the vowel sound that follows the consonants z, c and s.

Nasal vowel

ong

o -ng          ong

## 3. Tones:

During actual communication the tones of certain syllables in the language flow will undergo some changes, which we call tonal changes. Here we will first say something about the changes of the third tone, which you have already come across in the first four lessons.

The third tone syllables should be pronounced as a falling-rising tone when it is read by itself, or when it is used at the end of a word or sentence. For example:

    shǒu        wòshǒu

    nǐ          xièxie nǐ

But if a third tone syllable appears before another third tone syllable, the former should be pronounced as a rising tone, similar to the second tone rather than a falling-rising tone. For example:

```
          5
         4
         3
         2
         1
```

    nǐ hǎo          shǒubiǎo
                    wristwatch

When a third tone syllable appears before the first, second, fourth or toneless syllables, it should be pronounced as a low falling tone, or the first half of the falling-rising tone. For example:

nǚ rén                            lǎo rén

hǎo shū                          hǎo cài
(good book)

nǐmen

4. Vis-à-vis English pronunciation:

zh   Its near equivalent is [dʒ] as in *joy* and *judge*. Zh in standard Chinese is
     pronounced without rounding and protruding the lips.

ch   Its near equivalent is [tʃ] as in *child* and *lunch*. Ch in standard Chinese is
     pronounced without rounding and protruding the lips.

c    Its equivalent is [t] and [s] combined as in *cats* and *bits*.

s    Its eqivalent is [s] as in *see* and *sun*.

k    Its equivalent is [k] as in *key* and *kite*.

### Exercises

1. Read aloud the following initials and finals:
   zh   ch   c   s   k
   ong

2. Read aloud the following:
   zhī   chī   shī   rī   zī   cī   sī
   kē   hē   zhōng   chōng   chā   kā   sān   shān
   guō   kuō   cài   zài
   míng   yíng   líng   níng

3. Tone discrimination:
   hǎo   nǐhǎo   nǐmen hǎo
   lǎo   niánlǎo

hǎo tiān    hǎo rén    hǎo xì

lǎoshǔ           lǎohǔ          jiǔ

rat, mouse          tiger          liquor, wine

4. Learn and read aloud new words:

   (1) Look at the following pictures and fill in the blanks with nouns:

_____    _____       _____       _____

   (2) Look at the following pictures and fill in the blanks with verbs:

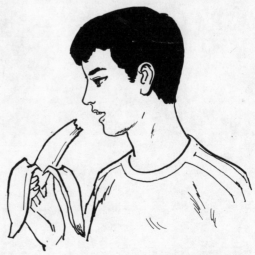

_____                  _____

## 5. Substitution drills:

(1) Zhè shì shénme?

Zhè shì

(2) Nà shì shénme?

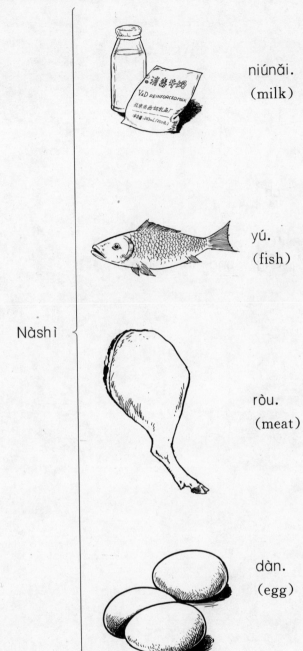

niúnǎi.
(milk)

yú.
(fish)

Nàshì

ròu.
(meat)

dàn.
(egg)

（3）

$$
\left.\begin{array}{l} Wǒ \\ Nǐ \\ Tā \end{array}\right\} \begin{array}{l} chī \\ hē \end{array} \left\{\begin{array}{l} niúnǎi. \\ chá. \\ kāfēi. \\ yú. \\ ròu. \\ dàn. \\ sānmíngzhì. \\ Zhōngguó cài. \end{array}\right.
$$

6. Sound discrimination:

b　p　d　t　zh　ch　z　c

zh　z　ch　c　sh　s

j　q　g　k　l　n

u　ü　e　o　en　eng　ong　in　ing

# Summary (Lessons 1-4)

1. The alphabet

| Capital letter | Small letter | Pronun-ciation | | Capital letter | Small letter | Pronun-ciation |
|---|---|---|---|---|---|---|
| A | a | a | | N | n | nê |
| B | b | bê | | O | o | o |
| C | c | cê | | P | p | pê |
| D | d | dê | | Q | q | qiu |
| E | e | e | | R | r | ar |
| F | f | êf | | S | s | ês |
| G | g | gê | | T | t | tê |
| H | h | ha | | U | u | u |
| I | i | i | | V* | v | vê |
| J | j | jie | | W | w | wa |
| K | k | kê | | X | x | xi |
| L | l | êl | | Y | y | ya |
| M | m | êm | | Z | z | zê |

  \* V is used only to spell foreign words and words from minority nationality languages and local dialects.

2. ABC song

      3 · 2 3 1 | 5 6 5 - | 6 · 5 3 5 | 2 3 2 - |
      a  b c d  e f g,   h  i j k  l m n,

      5 3 5  0 | 1 5 6  0 | 5 6 3  - | 2 3 1  - |
      o p q,   r s t,    u v w    x y z.

3. Table of initials (consonants placed at the beginning of each Chinese syllable)

| | Pronun-ciation | | Pronun-ciation | | Pronun-ciation |
|---|---|---|---|---|---|
| b | bo | g | ge | zh | zhi |
| p | po | k | ke | ch | chi |
| m | mo | h | he | sh | shi |
| f | fo | j | ji | r | ri |
| d | de | q | qi | z | zi |
| t | te | x | xi | c | ci |
| n | ne | | | s | si |
| l | le | | | | |

## 4. The articulation of initials

| initial / manner of articulation — points of articulation | plosive voiceless unaspirated | plosive voiceless aspirated | fricative voiceless | fricative voiced | africate voiceless unaspirated | africate voiceless aspirated | nasal voiced | lateral voiced |
|---|---|---|---|---|---|---|---|---|
| bilabial { upper lip / lower lip | b | p | | | | | m | |
| labio-dental { upper dental / lower dental | | | f | | | | | |
| blade-alveolar { blade narrow passage between teeth | | | s | | z | c | | |
| alveolar { blade / upper gum | d | t | | | | | n | l |
| blade-palatal { blade front / hard palate | | | sh | r | zh | ch | | |
| blade { blade / hard palate | | | x | | j | q | | |
| velar { velar / soft palate | g | k | h | | | | | |

## 5. Table of finals (finals are vowels placed after initials, or phoneme groups centring around vowels)

| | i | u | ü |
|---|---|---|---|
| a | ia | ua | |
| o | | uo | |
| e | | | |
| ê | ie | | üe |
| -i (as in zi, ci, si) | | | |
| -i (as in zhi, chi shi, ri) | | | |
| er | | | |
| ai | | uai | |
| ei | | uei | |
| ao | iao | | |
| ou | iou | | |
| an | ian | uan | üan |
| en | in | uen | ün |
| ang | iang | uang | |
| eng | ing | ueng | |
| ong | iong | | |

Note:

In the first four lessons all the simple vowels and a number of compound vowels have been introduced. The above table will enable you to spell and pronounce all the vowel sounds in standard Chinese.

6. Rules of spelling

(1) The -i in zhi, chi, shi, ri, zi, ci, si is not pronounced as i. The -i stands for the vowel sounds that follow the consonants zh, ch, sh, r, z, c, s.

(2) The retroflex vowel er (its manner of articulation is similar to the central vowel e though the tongue is rolled up without touching the upper palate) is written as er when it forms a syllable by itself; it is written as -r when used as a terminal sound. For example: huār.

(3) The -e in ie and ue is written as ê if it stands alone. This is to differentiate it from e.

(4) When the finals that begin with i form syllables by themselves, they are written as yi, ya, ye, yao, you, yan, yin, yang, ying, yong. The purpose is to draw a clear distinction between different syllables so that the i is not taken as part of the foregoing syllable. For example: āyí, ài.

(5) By the same token when the finals that begin with u form syllables by themselves, they are written as wu, wa, wo, wai, wei, wan, wen, wang, weng.

(6) When the finals that begin with ü form syllables by themselves they are written as yu, yue, yuan, yun, omitting the umlaut on ü. When these vowels combine with j, q and x to form syllables, the umlaut is also omitted. For example: ju, qu, xu, xuan, xun.

(7) When combined with initials, iou, uei and uen are written as iu, ui, un. For example: jiu, hui, gun.

7. Tones

| first tone | second tone | third tone | fourth tone |
|---|---|---|---|
| ā | á | ǎ | à |
| mā | má | mǎ | mà |
| tāng | táng | tǎng | tàng |
| yī | yí | yǐ | yì |

yuān　　　　　yuán　　　　　yuǎn　　　　　yuàn

Zhōng wén yǔ diào (tones in Chinese)

yōu yáng měi miào (melodious and beautiful)

yīn yáng shǎng qù (high and level, rising, falling-rising, falling)

shān míng shuǐ xiù (green hills and clear waters)

huā hóng liǔ lǜ (red flowers and green willows)

xīn míng yǎn liàng (see and think clearly)

dōu néng lǐng huì (everyone can understand)

fēi cháng hǎo jì (very easy to memorize)

Note: No tone marks appear on toneless syllables.

8. A summary of difficult sounds in Chinese

Native speakers of English need to pay special attention to the pronunciation of j, q and x, because there are no equivalents in the English phonetics system. Imitate these sounds by listening carefully to your teacher or tape recording.

Zh, ch, sh and r also need special attention not to pronounce them with rounded and protruded lips.

Read aloud the following syllables:

| | | | | | | |
|---|---|---|---|---|---|---|
| jìjié | jiéjú | jùjué | jíjù | jiānjù | jiāojù | jiějué |
| jūnjiàn | jīngjù | jiājǐn | jǐnjí | jiǔjīn | juéjìn | |
| qīqiào | qiānqiáng | qìqiú | quángqín | qǔqīn | qīnqì | |
| qíjì | quánjī | qiánjìn | quēxí | qièjì | qíngjǐng | qiújìn |
| xuéxí | xìnxī | xiāoxi | xiūxié | xióngxīn | xíngxīng | |
| xiūxi | xiùjué | xiángxì | xiānjìn | xuéqī | xūnjī | xiāojìn |
| zhīzhū | zhòngzhí | zhírì | zhǔchí | zhuānzhì | zhōngshí | |
| chéngchí | chǎnchú | chéngshì | chǒngrǔ | chǔnzhū | chánchú | |
| shūshu | shēnshì | shīrén | shuàizhì | shēchǐ | shōushi | |
| ruǎnruò | rěnràng | ruòzhì | róurèn | rènshū | ròucháng | |

# Lesson Five

## Text

△: Qǐngwèn, nín guìxìng?

May I know your name, please?

○: Wǒ xìng Lǐ, jiào Lǐ Níng.

My surname is Li. I'm called Li Ning.

△: Lī Nìng?

Lī Nìng?

○: Bú shì Lī Nìng, shì Lǐ Níng.

It's not Lī Nìng, but Lǐ Níng.

△: Lǐ Níng?

Lǐ Níng?

○: Hǎo, hěn hǎo.

Good. Very good.

## Vocabulary

| | | |
|---|---|---|
| Qǐngwèn | | please tell me, may I ask |
| wèn | *v.* | ask |
| guìxìng | | surname |
| xìng | *v.* | surname, to be sur-named |
| jiào | *v.* | to be called |
| bù | | no, not |
| hěn | *ad.* | very |

## Explanations of the Text

"Qǐngwèn, nín guìxìng?" is the most frequent expression used by Chinese people when they meet for the first time. Guì has the meaning of respectable and noble. The whole sentence shows politeness and courtesy. Generally, people respond to this question in three ways:

1. Wǒ xìng Lǐ, jiào Lǐ Níng.
2. Wǒ jiào Lǐ Níng.
3. Wǒ xìng Lǐ.

At their first meeting, people may feel there is no need to tell their whole name and may simply tell his/her surname to the other person.

## Sentence Patterns

Nín guì xìng?

Wǒ xìng Lǐ,      jiào Lǐ Níng.

  Zhāng,      Zhāng Fāng.

  Wáng,      Wáng Xiǎopéng.

## Exercises

1. Pronounce the following syllables:

| | | | |
|---|---|---|---|
| bū | bú | bǔ | bù |
| lī | lí | lǐ | lì |
| qīng | qíng | qǐng | qìng |
| xīng | xíng | xǐng | xìng |
| wēn | wén | wěn | wèn |
| hāo | háo | hǎo | hào |
| shī | shí | shǐ | shì |
| guī | | guǐ | guì |
| | nín | | |
| | hén | hěn | hèn |

2. Read aloud the following words (pay attention to changes in the third tone):

Lǐ Níng    qǐngwèn

hǎo    hěn hǎo

wǒ xìng Lǐ

3. Fill in the blanks：

    （1）Qǐngwèn，_____ guìxìng?

        Wǒ _____ Shǐmìsī，_____ Wēilián·Shǐmìsī.

    （2）Qǐngwèn，nín _____?

        Wǒ xìng _____，jiào _____.

4. Make sentences：

    （1）guìxìng    nín    qǐngwèn

    （2）Gélín    xìng    wǒ

    （3）jiào    wǒ    Sūshān

    （4）shénme    tā    jiào

5. Conversation：

Talk with fellow students，asking each other's names.

# Lesson Six

## Text

△: Nǐ jiào shénme míngzi?

What's your name?

○: Wǒ jiào Bǐdé, tā jiào Sūshān.

My name is Peter. She is called Susan.

△: Nǐmen hǎo! Wǒ jiào Zhāng Fāng, shì lǎoshī.

How do you do! I'm called Zhang Fang, a teacher.

○: Fāng lǎoshī, nín hǎo!

How do you do, Teacher Fang.

△: Bú duì, Fāng shì míng, Zhāng shì xìng.

That's not correct. Fang is my given name. My surname is Zhang.

○: Duìbuqǐ! Zhāng lǎoshī, nín hǎo!

I am sorry. Teacher Zhang, how do you do!

△: Duì le! Nǐ hěn cōngming.

That's right. You are very bright.

## Vocabulary

| | | | | | | |
|---|---|---|---|---|---|---|
| míngzi | *n.* | name | duì | *a.* | right, correct | |
| míng | *n.* | given name | le | | (a modal particle | |
| xìng | *n.* | surname | | | used at the end of a | |
| lǎoshī | *n.* | teacher | | | sentence showing | |
| cōngming | *a.* | bright, intelligent | | | affirmation) | |

## Explanations of the Text

"Nǐ jiào shénme míngzi?" is an informal expression generally used when a teacher is talking to his/her student, or an elderly person is addressing a younger person. In a situation in which politeness and courtesy are required, this expression must not be used. Instead, one should say:"Nín guìxìng?"

## Sentence Patterns

1. Nǐ ⎫
   Tā ⎭ jiào shénme míngzi?

   Wǒ ⎫        ⎧ Zhāng Fāng.
   Tā ⎭ jiào ⎨ Bǐdé.
              ⎪ Sūshān.
              ⎩ Wēilián · Shǐmìsī.

2. Nǐ
   Tā
   Sūshān ⎬ hěn cōngming.
   Bǐdé

## Exercises

1. Pronounce the following syllables:

   nī      ní      nǐ      nì
   bū      bú      bǔ      bù
   lāo     láo     lǎo     lào
   jiāo    jiáo    jiǎo    jiào
   shān    shán    shǎn    shàn
   fāng    fáng    fǎng    fàng
           míng    mǐng    mìng
   duī                     duì

2. Read aloud the following words paying attention to toneless syllables:

   tāmen    nǐmen    wǒmen
   shénme   cōngming   míngzi
   duìbuqǐ   duì le

3. Read aloud the following difficult sounds:

   sh—s                    zh—z

| shī | shí | shǐ | shì | zhī | zhí | zhǐ | zhì |
|-----|-----|-----|-----|-----|-----|-----|-----|
| shēn | shén | shěn | shèn | zhōu | zhóu | zhǒu | zhòu |
| shān | | shǎn | shàn | zhān | | zhǎn | zhàn |
| sū | sú | | sù | zī | | zǐ | zì |

4. Look at the following pictures and tell their names:

Zhuóbiélín
(Chaplin)

Bèilì
(Pele)

Línkěn
(Lincoln)

Pǐnuòcáo
(Pinocchio)

Wéinàsī
(Venus)

Āfántí
(Nasredin)

5. Fill in the blanks:

   (1) Wǒ jiào Zhāng Fāng,

      Zhāng shì _____, Fāng shì _____.

   (2) Tā jiào Lǐ Níng,

      Lǐ shì _____, Níng shì _____.

   (3) Tā jiào Wēilián·Shǐmìsī,

      _____ shì xìng, _____ shì míng.

   (4) Wǒ jiào _____,

xìng shì _____, míng shì _____.

6. Dialogue:

   Nǐ xìng shénme? Jiào shénme míngzi?

   Wǒ xìng _____, jiào _____.

   _____ shì xìng, _____ shì míng.

7. Conversation (students introduce themselves).

# Lesson Seven

## Text

△: Qǐngwèn, nǐ shì nǎ guó rén?

Excuse me, what is your nationality?

○: Wǒ shì Měiguó rén, nǐ shì nǎ guó rén?

I am American. What's your nationality?

△: Wǒ shì Rìběn rén.

I am Japanese.

○: Nǐ de Hànyǔ hěn hǎo.

You speak Chinese very well.

△: Wǒ zài Běijīng xué guo Hànyǔ.

I have studied Chinese in Beijing.

○: Wǒ yě zài Běijīng xué guo Hànyǔ.

I have also studied Chinese in Beijing.

△: Ò, shìjiè zhēn xiǎo!

Oh. It's really a small world!

## Vocabulary

| | | | | | |
|---|---|---|---|---|---|
| guó | *n.* | country, state | xiǎo | *a.* | small |
| Hànyǔ | *n.* | the Chinese language | xué | *v.* | study, learn |
| | | | zài | *prep.* | at (before time or place) |
| shìjiè | *n.* | world | | | |
| nǎ | *pro.* | where | yě | *ad.* | too, also |

| | | | | |
|---|---|---|---|---|
| zhēn | *ad*. | really | ò | oh (interjection) |
| guo | | (auxiliary word used | Měiguó | U.S.A. |
| | | after a verb to show | Rìběn | Japan |
| | | that some time has | Běijīng | (capital of China) |
| | | passed between the | | |
| | | time of action and | | |
| | | now) | | |

## Explanations of the Text

1. According to Chinese custom, if a country has a one-syllable name, it must be followed by the syllable guó. For example: Zhōngguó, Měiguó. Two-syllable and multi-syllable names do not take on guó. For example: Rìběn, Xībānyá (Spain), Aòdàlìyà (Australia).

2. In Chinese, the prepositional phrases or adverbs modifying verbal predicates are placed before the verbs. For example:

Wǒ <u>yě</u>    <u>zài Běijīng</u> xué guo Hànyǔ.

    adverb   prepositional phrase

## Sentence Patterns

1. Qǐngwèn, nǐ shì nǎ guó rén?

Wǒ shì ⎰ Zhōngguó ⎱ rén.
        Měiguó
        Rìběn
        Yīngguó (Britain)

2. Nǐ (hěn) cōngming.

Shìjiè (zhēn) xiǎo.

(Nǐ de) Hànyǔ (hěn) hǎo.

3.

$$\text{Wǒ zài} \begin{cases} \text{Zhōngguó} \\ \text{Měiguó} \\ \text{Rìběn} \\ \text{Éluósī (Russia)} \end{cases} \text{xué guo} \begin{cases} \text{Hànyǔ.} \\ \text{Yīngyǔ (English).} \\ \text{Rìyǔ (Japanese).} \\ \text{Éyǔ (Russian).} \end{cases}$$

**Exercises**

1. Pronounce the following syllables:

| nā | ná | nǎ | nà |
|---|---|---|---|
| guō | guó | guǒ | guò |
| mēi | méi | měi | mèi |
| hān | hán | hǎn | hàn |
| yū | yú | yǔ | yù |
| āo | áo | ǎo | ào |

2. Read aloud the following (paying attention to tones):

Hànyǔ      xué Hànyǔ      yě xué Hànyǔ

shìjiè      shìjiè zhēn xiǎo

Běijīng      Běijīng rén      zài Běijīng

xué      xué guo      xué guo Yīngyǔ

3. Tone discrimination:

nǎ      nà      Hànyǔ      Hán Yù

Běijīng      bèijǐng

shìjiè      shìjié      shíjié

shījiě      shǐjié      shìjiē

4. Memorize the following words:

Měiguó          Rìběn          Zhōngguó

shìjiè                          Běijīng

5. Fill in the blanks：

   （1）Nǐ shì _____ guó rén?

      Wǒ _____ Měiguó rén.

   （2）Fill in blanks with nǎ or nà：

      _____ shì shénme?

      _____ shì kāfēi.

      Nǐ shì _____ guó rén?

      Tā shì _____ guó rén?

6. Make sentences：

   （1）wǒ Hànyǔ xué guo Běijīng zài

   （2）hěn hǎo Hànyǔ de nǐ

   （3）pay attention to the use of yě

      （Nǐ shì Měiguó rén），wǒ shì Měiguó rén yě

      （Nǐ xìng Zhāng），wǒ Zhāng xìng yě

      （Nǐ shì lǎoshī），wǒ lǎoshī yě shì

7. Substitution drills：

   Qǐngwèn ⎰ nín guìxìng?
           ⎱ nǐ shì nǎ guó rén?
             nǐ jiào shénme míngzi?

8. Conversation：

   Ask about each other's nationality.

# Summary (Lessons 5-7)

## Communicative Expressions

1. Greeting expressions：

   Nǐ (men) hǎo!

   Nín hǎo!

   Qǐngwèn,…

   Huānyíng nǐ!

   Duìbuqǐ!

   Xièxie!

2. Asking about names：

   Q：Nín guìxìng?

   A：Wǒ xìng Zhāng, jiào Zhāng Fāng.

   Q：Nǐ jiào shénme míngzi?

   A：Wǒ jiào Lǐ Níng.

3. Asking about nationality：

   Q：Nǐ shì nǎ guó rén?

   A：Wǒ shì $\begin{cases} \text{Měiguó rén.} \\ \text{Rìběn rén.} \end{cases}$

## Introduction to Grammar

1. Chinese is a unique language. Anyone who learns it will find it difficult to really understand and master the language if he/she does not completely cast away the habits and concepts acquired from his/her mother tongue or other foreign languages.

   Languages can be compared and contrasted. Taking into account the linguistic habits which you have already acquired, we will explain the grammar of Chinese, starting with the similarities between Chinese and other languages. From similarities we will go on to differences; from the easy we will proceed to the difficult. We will try to help you learn the rudiments within a very short time and reduce the special difficulties for beginners.

2. The most prominent characteristic of Chinese is the fact that it is not inflectional. None of the words in Chinese has inflectional changes of gender, number, case or tense. For example, the word shi does not have personal change：

Nǐ(men)
Wǒ (men)  ⎫
Tā (men)  ⎭  shì Zhōngguó rén.

Shì is used without change in all three cases regardless of person or number. This freedom from inflection gives Chinese the advantage of simplicity. As soon as we have learned a certain number of words, we can combine them according to certain formulae to express ourselves and communicate with others. There is no need to memorize various rules governing inflection.

3. The communicative unit of Chinese is the sentence. Sentences in Chinese are quite different from those in other languages. However, the simple sentences that have been taught in the last three lessons are similar to those in other languages. They are composed of a topic (subject) and a declarative expression (predicate):

Topic (Subject)   Declarative   Expression (Predicate)
Nǐ                hǎo!
Shìjiè            [zhēn] xiǎo!
(Nǐ de) Hànyǔ     [hěn] hǎo.

Some predicates include two parts: verb (or a judgment expression) + associated elements (object). For example:

Subject              Predicate (Verb + Object)
Wǒ                   jiào Zhāng Fāng.
Wǒ                   shì Měiguó rén.
Wǒ [zài Běijīng]     xué guo Hànyǔ.

The syntactical order of the verb and its associated elements (objects) is the same as in European languages.

Special attention needs however to be paid to the grammatical terms used in this book: sentence, subject, predicate, verb, object. These terms used to refer to Chinese grammar are similar only in form to those in European languages; they may have very different meanings. Further explanations will be given as we proceed.

4. During communication, certain parts of a sentence may often be omitted. This is one of the differences between Chinese and other languages. For example:

Wǒ xìng Lǐ, (wǒ) jiào Lǐ Níng.

Wǒ jiào Zhāng Fāng, (wǒ) shì lǎoshī.

In both sentences, the words in the parenthesis are omitted without causing any confusion. Another example:

(     ) Bú shì Lǐ Níng, shì Lǐ Níng.

(     ) Bú duì, Fāng shì míng, Zhāng shì xìng.

In these two sentences, a pronoun is needed to precede the judgment expression (linking verb) as subject according to usages in European languages. In Chinese, however, it is often omitted. According to the Chinese custom of expression and mentality, it is quite acceptable to leave out the subject before the judgment expression as long as the meaning of the sentence is clear.

## Understanding China

### Chinese Names

Méi Lánfāng    Sūn Zhōngshān    Qián Xuésēn    Zhūgě Liàng

Sūn Wùkōng

A Chinese name is composed of two parts—a surname and a given name. The surname comes first, followed by the given name. Most surnames are monosyllabic. The most common surnames are Zhang, Wang, Li, Zhao and Liu. There are a few disyllabic surnames such as Zhuge, Ouyang and Shangguan. Given names can be either monosyllabic or disyllabic.

### Humour

1. Listen to the recording and fill in the blanks:

○: Nǐ hǎo! Nǐ jiào shénme míngzi?

44

△: Nǐ hǎo! Wǒ jiào Lǐ Bái　(a famous poet in ancient China).

　　Nǐ jiào shénme míngzi?

○: Wǒ jiào Shāshìbǐyà (Shakespeare).

　　Nǐ shì nǎ guó rén?

△: Wǒ shì Zhōngguó rén. Nǐ ne?

○: Wǒ shì Yīngguó rén.

Fill in the blanks:

○: Name: _____

　　Nationality: _____

△: Name: _____

　　Nationality: _____

2. Māma jiào shénme míngzi?

○: Xiǎo gūniang (girl), nǐ māma jiào shénme míngzi?

△: Wǒ māma míngzi hěn duō (many).

○: Wèishénme (why)?

△: Wǒ jiào tā "māma", nǎinai (grandmother) jiào tā "Huìfēn", bàba jiào tā "Wèi"(Hey, you)!

## Introduction to Chinese Characters

The Chinese written language is an ancient and unique writing system with a history of 6000 years. There are a total of 60,000 characters, of which only 3,000-4,500 are frequently used.

Ancient Chinese characters evolved from pictures:

| | |
|---|---|
| rì | sun |
| yuè | moon |
| shān | hill |
| shuǐ | water |
| huǒ | fire |
| yǔ | rain |
| chē | cart |
| zǐ | son |
| niú | ox |
| mǎ | horse |
| yú | fish |

# Lesson Eight

**Text**

△: Wáng lǎoshī, nín zǎo!

Good morning, teacher Wang!

○: Nǐ hǎo! Nǐ qù nǎr?

Hello! Where are you going?

△: Wǒ qù jiàoshì.

I am going to the classroom.

○: Nǐ chídào le, zuótiān wǎnshang tiàowǔ le?

You are late. Did you go dancing last night?

△: Zuótiān wǎnshang xuéxí le.

I studied last night.

○: Zhēnde ma?

Really?

## Vocabulary

| | | | | | |
|---|---|---|---|---|---|
| jiàoshì | *n.* | classroom | zǎo | *a.* | early |
| zuótiān | *n.* | yesterday | zhēnde | *a.* | real |
| wǎnshang | *n.* | night | qù | *v.* | to go to |
| nǎr (nǎ+er) | *pro.* | where | chídào | *v.* | to be late |

| tiàowǔ | v. | to dance | ma | (a modal particle generally |
|--------|----|----------|----|----------------------------|
| xuéxí  | v. | to study, to learn | | used with yes/no questions, |
| | | | | expressing interrogation) |

## Explanations of the Text

1. Le is a function word used at the end of a sentence. It not only expresses affirmity, but also shows that an event has occurred or a change has taken place. The le sentence in the text is an example of the occurrence of an event. For example:

$$\text{Zuótiān wǎnshang wǒ} \begin{cases} \text{tiàowǔ} \\ \text{xuéxí} \\ \text{hē chá} \\ \text{chī Zhōngguó cài} \end{cases} \text{le.}$$

2. Ma is a function word used at the end of a sentence expressing interrogation. It is used in yes/no sentences (questions). For example:

$$\begin{matrix} \text{Zhēnde} \\ \text{Shì (tā)} \end{matrix} \Big\} \text{ma?}$$

$$\text{Nǐ shì} \begin{cases} \text{Zhōngguó} \\ \text{Měiguó} \\ \text{Rìběn} \end{cases} \text{rén ma?}$$

3. Nǐ qù nǎr?

   Wǒ qù jiàoshì.

The syntactic order of these two sentences (a question and an answer) are identical. What should be noted is the placing of the interrogative pronoun after the verb. This order is very different from English. For example:

Where are you going?

## Sentence Patterns

1. $\begin{matrix} \text{Nín} \\ \text{Nǐ} \\ \text{Lǎoshī} \\ \text{Wáng lǎoshī} \end{matrix} \Big\} \text{zǎo!}$

2. $\begin{matrix} \text{Nín} \\ \text{Nǐ} \\ \text{Wǒ} \end{matrix} \Big\} \text{qù} \begin{cases} \text{nǎr?} \\ \text{jiàoshì.} \\ \text{Zhōngguó.} \\ \text{Měiguó.} \\ \text{Rìběn.} \end{cases}$

## Exercises

1. Read aloud the following syllables:

   wāng  wáng  wǎng  wàng

   lāo   láo   lǎo   lào

   shī   shí   shǐ   shì

   jiāo  jiáo  jiǎo  jiào

   tiāo  tiáo  tiǎo  tiào

   wū   wú   wǔ   wù

   xuē  xué  xuě  xuè

2. Read aloud the following paying attention to third tone changes and toneless syllables:

   Wáng lǎoshī     nín zǎo     nǐ hǎo

   tiàowǔ          nǐ qù nǎr    wǎnshang

   nǐ chídào le    zhēnde ma

3. Tone discrimination:

   nǎ+er — nǎr   nà+er — nàr (there)

   jiàoshì   jiàoshī (teacher)

4. Memorize the following words:

lǎoshī

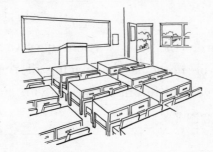

jiàoshì

tiàowǔ

xuéxí

5. Fill in the blanks with ma or le (sometimes neither is needed):

    (1) Nǐ qù nǎr ( )?

    (2) Zhēnde ( )?

    (3) Nǐ shì nǎ guó rén ( )?

    (4) Nǐ shì Rìběn rén ( )?

    (5) Nǐ qù nǎr ( )?

        Wǒ qù jiàoshì ( ).

    (6) Nǐ zuótiān qù nǎr ( )?

        Wǒ zuótiān qù jiàoshì ( ).

    (7) Wǒ zuótiān wǎnshang tiàowǔ ( ).

6. The following are a few commonly used interrogative sentence patterns with the same word order: subject (noun or pronoun), predicate (verb or judgment expression) and object (interrogative pronoun or interrogative pronoun + noun). Please make sentences according to the order of subject, predicate and object:

| Subject | Predicate | Object |
| --- | --- | --- |
| nǐ | shì | shénme |
| tā | jiào | nǎr |
| Sūshān | qù | shuí |
| zhè | | shénme míngzi |
| nà | | nǎ guó rén |

    (1) _____ ?

    (2) _____ ?

    (3) _____ ?

    (4) _____ ?

    (5) _____ ?

    (6) _____ ?

    (7) _____ ?

    (8) _____ ?

    (9) _____ ?

    (10) _____ ?

7. Make sentences with the following verbs: chī, hē, qù, chídào, tiàowǔ, xuéxí with le at the end of the sentences:

    (1) _____    (4) _____

    (2) _____    (5) _____

    (3) _____    (6) _____

# Lesson Nine

## Text

△: Xiǎo Pān!

Xiao Pan!

○: Xià shīfu!

Mr. Xia!

△: Nǐ gànmá qù?

What are you going to do?

○: Wǒ shàngbān qù. Nín gànmá qù?

I am going to work. What are you going to do?

△: Yídàzǎo, chūqù liùliu.

I'm going out for a walk in the early morning (air).

○: Shēntǐ tǐng hǎo de?

Are you in very good health?

△: Hái còuhe.

Not too bad.

## Vocabulary

| | | | | | | |
|---|---|---|---|---|---|---|
| shīfu | *n.* | mister, master worker | | shēntǐ | *n.* | body, health |
| yídàzǎo | | early in the morning, | | gànmá | | do what |
| | | in the early morning | | shàngbān | *v.* | to go to work |

| | | | |
|---|---|---|---|
| chūqù | *v.* | to go out | |
| liùliu | *v.* | to take a walk | |
| còuhe | *a.* | not too bad | |
| tǐng | *ad.* | quite | |
| hái | *ad.* | still | |

de     (here de is a modal particle expressing judgment rather than an auxiliary showing affiliation or modification)

## Explanations of the Text

1. Among friends and acquaintances, the Chinese people often tend to add a word xiǎo before the surname of a young person. For example, Xiǎo Pān, Xiǎo Lǐ, Xiǎo Wáng. This form of address sounds informal and intimate.

2. Wǒ shàngbān qù. The predicate of this sentence pattern is verb + qù. It shows that someone is doing something or about to do something.

3. Wǒ chūqù liùliù. This sentence pattern connects two verbs to show that the two actions are performed one after the other. There are many examples like this:

Wǒ qù jiàoshì xuéxí.

Tā qù Měiguó xué Yīngyǔ.

Nǐ qù Rìběn xué Rìyǔ.

## Sentence Patterns

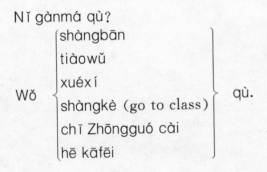

Nǐ gànmá qù?

Wǒ { shàngbān / tiàowǔ / xuéxí / shàngkè (go to class) / chī Zhōngguó cài / hē kāfēi } qù.

## Exercises

1. Read aloud the following syllables:

| | | | |
|---|---|---|---|
| xiāo | xiáo | xiǎo | xiào |
| xiā | xiá | | xià |
| pān | pán | | pàn |
| bān | | bǎn | bàn |
| qū | qú | qǔ | qù |

| | | | |
|---|---|---|---|
| zāo | záo | zǎo | zào |
| liū | liú | liǔ | liù |
| gān | | gǎn | gàn |
| tī | tí | tǐ | tì |
| tīng | tíng | tǐng | tìng |
| hāi | hái | hǎi | hài |

2. Read aloud the following words paying attention to third tone and toneless syllables:

Xiǎo Pān    yídàzǎo    tǐng hǎo

shēntǐ hǎo    shīfu    liùliu

tǐng hǎo de    hái còuhe

3. Sound discrimination drills (tongue twisters):

(1) Sì shí sì gè sè shìzi.

(44 puckery persimmons)

(2) Sì shì sì, shí shì shí, shí sì shì shí sì, sì shí shì sì shí.

(4 is 4; 10 is 10; 14 is 14; 40 is 40. )

4. Memorize the following new words:

shīfu    gànmá    shàngbān    yídàzǎo

chūqù    qù    shēntǐ    tǐng

hái    còuhe    xuéxí    jiàoshì

5. Fill in the blanks:

(1) Nín gànmá qù?

Yídàzǎo, (      )chūqù liùliu.

(2) (      )shēntǐ tǐng hǎo de?

(      )hái còuhe.

(3) Tā qù nǎr le?

(      )qù jiàoshì xuéxí le.

6. Make sentences:

(1) gànmá    nǐ    qù

(2) shàngkè    qù    wǒ

(3) liùliu    wǒ    chūqù

(4) Hànyǔ    xuéxí    wǒ    Zhōngguó    qù

(5) Rìběn    Rìyǔ    tā    xué    qù

7. Substitution drills:

(1) Q: Nǐ shēntǐ hǎo ma?

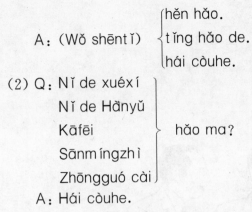

A：(Wǒ shēntǐ) 
- hěn hǎo.
- tǐng hǎo de.
- hái còuhe.

(2) Q：
- Nǐ de xuéxí
- Nǐ de Hǎnyǔ
- Kāfēi
- Sānmíngzhì
- Zhōngguó cài

hǎo ma?

A：Hái còuhe.

(3) 

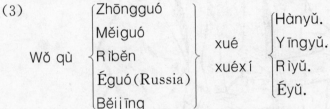

Wǒ qù
- Zhōngguó
- Měiguó
- Rìběn
- Éguó (Russia)
- Běijīng

xué
xuéxí
- Hànyǔ.
- Yīngyǔ.
- Rìyǔ.
- Éyǔ.

8. Translate the following sentences into Chinese:

(1) I am British. My last name is Smith. My first name is John.

(2) I have been to China.

(3) Chinese friends welcomed me.

(4) I have studied Chinese in Beijing.

(5) He has had Chinese tea, he also has had Chinese food.

# Lesson Ten

**Text**

△ : Lǎo Liú !

　　Lao Liu !

○ : Shì nín a , Wáng xiānsheng .

　　Hi ! It's you , Mr . Wang !

△ : Hǎo jiǔ bú jiàn , nǐ hǎo ma ?

　　Haven't seen you for a long time . How are you ?

○ : Mǎmahūhū . Nín ne ?

　　Just so - so . And you ?

△ : Hái nàyàng .

　　Just as before .

○ : Nín fūren ne ?

　　Where is your wife ? ( How is your wife ? )

△ : Tā qù Shànghǎi le .

　　She's gone to Shanghai .

○ : Háizi ne ?

　　And your child ?

△ : Wǒ guǎn a .

　　I am taking care of him ( her ) .

○ : Nín shòu le .

　　You've lost weight .

△ : Yòu dāng bàba yòu dāng mā , hái néng bú shòu ?

I have to play the role of both father and mother . How can I not lose weight ?

## Vocabulary

| | | | | | |
|---|---|---|---|---|---|
| xiānsheng | *n.* | Mister | dāng | *v.* | to be (play the role of) |
| fūren | *n.* | wife , Mrs. | néng | *v.* | to be able to |
| háizi | *n.* | child | hǎo | *ad.* | very |
| mā(māma) | *n.* | mother | yòu | *ad.* | at the same time , and |
| nàyàng | | of that kind | a | | interjection |
| jiǔ | *a.* | long (time) | ne | | a modal particle often |
| shòu | *a.* | thin | | | used in elliptical ques- |
| mǎmahūhū | *a.* | just so-so | | | tions |
| jiàn | *v.* | see | Shànghǎi | | a large city in east-cen- |
| guǎn | *v.* | to take care of | | | tral China |

## Explanations of the Text

1 . The manner of communication introduced in Lesson Ten is a very popular one among friends and acquaintances in China . It is intimate and informal in style and therefore would be inappropriate on formal and serious social occasions .

2 . Adding the word lǎo to a surname is an informal and intimate form of addressing an older person . In order to be polite and respectful , the word xiānsheng is placed after the surname , or the person's profession should be attached to the surname . For example : Zhāng lǎoshī ( teacher ) , Wáng shīfu ( master worker ) . There are also cases in which someone's position or title is placed after the surname . We will explain this form of address later .

3 . Yòu ··· yòu ··· is a pattern showing that two things are being done simultaneously . This should be differentiated from the pattern chūqù liùliù taught in the last lesson . The latter shows that two things are done one after the other .

4 . " Ne ? " is different from " ma ? " in that " ma ? " is used in yes / no questions , whereas " ne ? " is used in WH questions , for which " yes " or " no " does not suffice and detailed answers are required . For example :

55

—Nǐ shì Rìběn rén ma?

—Shì de.

—Nǐ shì nǎ guó rén ne?

—Wǒ shì Rìběn rén.

In addition, "ne?" is also often used in elliptical questions. For example:

Wǒ shì Rìběn rén, nǐ (shì nǎ guó rén) ne?

—Nǐ hǎo ma?

—Mǎmahūhū. Nín ne?

## Sentence Patterns

1.

$$\text{Hǎo jiǔ bú jiàn,} \begin{cases} \text{nín} \\ \text{nǐ} \\ \text{nǐ shēntǐ} \\ \text{nǐ fūrén} \\ \text{nǐ bàba} \\ \text{nǐ māma} \end{cases} \text{hǎo ma?}$$

2. Hǎo jiǔ bú jiàn, nǐ hǎo ma?

$$\text{(Wǒ)} \begin{cases} \text{hěn hǎo.} \\ \text{tǐng hǎo de.} \\ \text{hái nàyàng.} \\ \text{hái còuhe.} \\ \text{mǎmahūhū.} \end{cases}$$

## Exercises

1. Pronounce the following syllables:

| liū | liú | liǔ | liù |
|------|------|------|------|
| xiān | xián | xiǎn | xiàn |
| shēng | shéng | shěng | shèng |
| yāng | yáng | yǎng | yàng |
| yōu | yóu | yǒu | yòu |
| shōu | shóu | shǒu | shòu |

2. Read aloud the following words paying attention to toneless syllables:

xiānsheng    fūren    háizi

bàba    mǎmahūhū    nín    shòu - le

nǐ hǎo ma    nǐ fūren ne

3. Memorize the following new words:

xiānsheng    hǎo    jiǔ    jiàn
mǎmahūhū    nàyàng    fūren háizi
guǎn    shòu    dāng    néng

4. Fill in the blanks with ma or ne:

（1）Nǐ chī Zhōngguó cài（    ）?

（2）Nǐ chī shénme（    ）?

（3）Nǐ jiào shénme míngzi（    ）?

（4）Nín shì lǎoshī（    ）?

（5）Nǐ shì Měiguó rén（    ）?

（6）Wǒ shì Měiguó rén，nǐ（    ）?

（7）Zhōngguó chá hǎo hē（    ）?

（8）Tā zài nǎr（    ）?

5. Substitution drills:

Q：
　　　　⎧ fūren
　　　　⎪ háizi
　　Nǐ ⎨ bàba    ⎬  ne?
　　　　⎪ māma
　　　　⎩ péngyou

A：
　　　　　⎧ Shànghǎi
　　　　　⎪ Zhōngguó
　　Tā qù ⎨ Měiguó    ⎬  le.
　　　　　⎪ Rìběn
　　　　　⎩ jiàoshì

6. How should we address the following according to Chinese custom?

Tā xìng Lǐ.    Tā xìng Wáng.    Tā xìng Zhāng.    Tā jiào Shǐmìsī.

_____    _____    _____    _____

7. Make sentences with the following verbs，using the yòu … yòu pattern:

（1）

$$\text{hē}\begin{cases}\text{chá}\\\text{kāfēi}\\\text{niúnǎi}\\\text{shuǐ}\end{cases}, \quad \text{chī}\begin{cases}\text{sānmíngzhì}\\\text{Zhōngguó cài}\\\text{ròu}\\\text{dàn}\\\text{yú}\end{cases}.$$

（2）xuéxí，kàn（look，watch）diànshì（television）

（3）xǐhuān（like，love）bàba，xǐhuān māma

8．Translate the following sentences into Chinese：

（1）Please tell me who he is.

（2）It is no good to be careless in one's study.

（3）I am going to China to learn Chinese！

（4）He has to play the role of both father and mother.

（5）You have lost weight.

# Summary（Lessons 8-10）

## Communicative Expressions

How to greet people :

1. Q： Nǐ qù nǎr ?

   A： Wǒ qù { jiàoshì.
   bàngōngshì (office)
   shāngdiàn (store).

   Q： Nǐ gànmá qù ?

   A： Wǒ { shàngbān
   kàn diànshì
   xuéxí
   tiàowǔ } qù .

These two groups of sentences are common greeting expressions used between old acquaintances who often see each other . People who ask these questions do not really want to know where the other person is going or what he or she is going to do . These expressions simply show the speaker's concern about the person spoken to . The latter may tell the former what he or she is going to do , or he / she may not give a direct answer , but simply give a vague reply : Wǒ chūqù ( to go out ). Wǒ yǒu diǎnr shì ( I have something to do ).

2. Q： Hǎo jiǔ bú jiàn, nǐ { (shēntǐ) hǎo ma?
   tǐng hǎo de?
   fūren (háizi) hǎo ma?

   A： Wǒ { (shēntǐ)
   fūren
   háizi } { hěn hǎo.
   tǐng hǎo de.
   hái nàyàng.
   hái còuhe.
   mǎmahūhū.

These greeting expressions are used between friends or acquaintances who do not see each other often , showing the speaker's concern about the person spoken to or about his / her family members . Usually one should ask first about the person spoken to and then about his / her family members . The person spoken to can answer hěnhǎo . Sometimes one could say hái còuhe to show one has made no significant progress since they last met and there is nothing special worth mentioning. People use this expression to show modesty, for which the Chinese people are especially noted in their communication.

3. A: Nǐ zǎo (a)!

    B: Nǐ zǎo!

It is an old Chinese custom to get up early in the morning. When people meet at 5-7 am, they often say Nǐ zǎo to each other, implying an admiration for the other person's diligence and good habit. Nowadays, owing to the influence of foreign languages in China, some people often say Nǐ zǎo or Zǎoshang (morning) hǎo when they meet at 8 or 9 am.

4. A: Nǐ hǎo!

    B: Nǐ hǎo!

As a result of the influence of foreign languages in China, people now say Nǐ hǎo to both their acquaintances and strangers.

## Introduction to Grammar

1. As has been explained before, the judgment expression shì does not have conjugations. In interrogative sentences, the interrogative pronoun is placed after, rather than before, the word shì. This syntactic order is different from many other languages. For example:

Nǐ shì shuí?

Zhè shì shénme?

2. Verb or verbal phrase + qù shows that someone is doing or is going to do something. For example:

Wǒ shàngbān qù.

Tā tiàowǔ qù.

3. Yòu... yòu... shows that two actions are being performed at the same time (yòu should be followed by a verb). For example:

Wǒ yòu dāng bàba yòu dāng mā.

Wáng xiānsheng yòu guǎn háizi yòu shàngbān.

4. In the sentence Nǐ shòu le, the word shòu has two meanings and two usages:

One is static description: Nǐ hěn shòu.

The other expresses a kind of change: Nǐ shòu le.

The shòu in these two sentences are not at all the same in meaning and usage though they take the same form. This phenomenon is very common with nouns, verbs and adjectives.

## Understanding China

### Appellations in China

1. In China, people seldom address each other by his / her full name, except on very rare occasions, e. g. when an elder member of a family addresses a younger member, or between very good friends.

2. Between acquaintances and colleagues, a younger person is addressed as xiǎo + surname, and an elderly person is addressed as lǎo + surname. A tall person is addressed as dà ( big ) + surname ( for example : Dà Liú, Dà Lǐ ). These forms of appellation sound intimate and informal.

3. Surname + profession or position shows the speaker's respect for the person spoken to and connotes a sense of politeness and propriety.

4. The Chinese people also use tóngzhì ( comrade ) to address each other, but the scope of its usage is being reduced gradually. The terms that for a long time were not used frequently such as xiānsheng, fūren, xiǎojiě ( miss ) are being used more often these days.

5. Surname + gōng or lǎo is used to address an elderly learned person in high social position to show special respect. For example : Zhōu Gōng, Lǐ Lǎo.

## Humour

1. Gànmá qù ?

61

△ : Ê! Nǐ diào yú qù a?     A : Hi! Are you going fishing?

○ : Bù! Wǒ diào yú qù.     B : No, I'm going fishing.

△ : Ò, wǒ dàng nǐ diào yú qù ne.     A : Oh, I thought you were going fishing.

2. Tā shì shuí?

Tā bú shì wǒ de gēge, bú shì wǒ de dìdi, bú shì wǒ de jiějie (elder sister), yě bú shì wǒ de mèimei (younger sister), kě (but) tā shì wǒ bàba māma de háizi.

Tā shì shuí? Tā jiù (an adverb emphasizing the certainty of judgment) shì wǒ.

3. A Song of numerals

1 (yī)   2 (èr)   3 (sān)   4 (sì)   5 (wǔ)   6 (liù)   7 (qī)   8 (bā)   9 (jiǔ)   10 (shí).

1 2 3 4 5 6 7, wǒ de péngyou zài ( *v.* to be at ) nǎli (where)? 7 6 5 4 3 2 1, zài xuéxiào (school), zài jiāli (at home), wǒ de péngyou zài zhèli (here).

## Introduction to Chinese Characters

Some Chinese characters are formed by adding symbols to the original pictograph to focus on a particular part of the picture, or to designate a particular thing.

| | | | |
|---|---|---|---|
| 木 | 本 | běn | (the root of a plant) |
| 木 | 末 | mò | (the top of a plant) |
| 禾 | 禾 | hé | (the drooping ears of wheat or rice) |
| 刃 | 刃 | rèn | (the edge of a knife) |
| 甘 | 甘 | gān | (something delicious, sweet) |
| 二 | 上 | shàng | (above a horizontal line) |
| 二 | 下 | xià | (below a horizontal line) |
| 出 | 出 | chū | (a footprint outside a cave, meaning: be out) |

# Lesson Eleven

**Text**

△ : Qǐngwèn , zhèr dào nán shān duō yuǎn ?

Excuse me , how far is it to the South Hills ?

○ : Sān gōnglǐ .

Three kilometres .

△ : Kěyǐ dā chē ma ?

Could you give me a ride ?

○ : Shànglai ba !

Hop in !

△ : Xiànzài dào nán shān duō yuǎn ?

How far is it to the South Hills now ?

○ : Liù gōnglǐ .

Six kilometres .

△ : Shénme ?

I beg your pardon ?

○ : Wǒ de chē qù běi shān .

I am heading for the North Hills .

△ : Ā ?

Oh ?

# Vocabulary

| | | | | | | |
|---|---|---|---|---|---|---|
| nán | *n.* | south | sān | *n.* | three |
| shān | *n.* | hill | liù | *n.* | six |
| chē | *n.* | vehicle | duō | *a. ad.* | many, how many |
| gōnglǐ | *n.* | kilometre | ǎ | | an exclamation word |
| xiànzài | *n.* | now | | | showing astonish- |
| běi | *n.* | north | | | ment |
| zhèr (zhè+er) | *n.* | here | ba | | an auxiliary word in- |
| yuǎn | *a.* | far | | | dicating the impera- |
| dào | *v.* | to go to | | | tive mood |
| kěyǐ | *v.* | can | | | |
| dā | *v.* | to take a ride | | | |
| shànglái | *v.* | to come up, to come on board (in actual speech, it is pro- nounced as "shànglai") | | | |

## Explanations of the Text

1. Ba is an auxiliary word showing request or order. For example:

    Shànglai ba!

    Hē chá ba!

    Chī diǎnr (点儿) cài ba!

2. A summary of auxiliary words indicating mood

    (1) Interrogative auxiliary words ma and ne:

    Ma is used at the end of a yes / no question. For example:

    (Zhè shì) zhēnde ma?

    Nǐ shì Déguó rén ma?

    Ne is used at the end of a special question. For example:

    Wǒ shì Měiguó rén, nǐ (shì nǎ guó rén) ne?

    Nín chī shénme ne?

    (2) Affirmative auxiliary words de and le:

    De is used in sentences of affirmative mood. For example:

    —Nǐ hǎo ma?

—Wǒ tǐng hǎo de.

—Nǐ shì Běijīng rén ma?

—Shì de.

Le shows affirmative mood, but it also indicates that a change has taken place. For example:

Zuótiān wǎnshang tiàowǔ le.

Tā qù Shànghǎi le.

## Sentence Patterns

A:

Qǐngwèn, zhèr dào

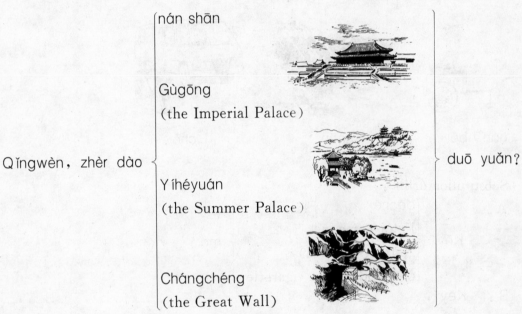

nán shān

Gùgōng
(the Imperial Palace)

Yíhéyuán
(the Summer Palace)

Chángchéng
(the Great Wall)

duō yuǎn?

B: Sān
Sì
Liù
Shí
......

gōnglǐ.

## Exercises

1. Read aloud the following syllables:

zhè + er — zhèr          huā (flower) + er — huār

nà + er — nàr            xiǎohái (child) + er — xiǎoháir

nǎ + er — nǎr            hòumén (backdoor) + er — hòuménr

2. Tone drills:

qǐngwèn    duō yuǎn    gōnglǐ    kěyǐ

běi shān    kěyǐ dā chē ma ?

shànglaiba    dào Běijīng le

3. Sound discrimination :

Sīrén ( private ) — shīrén ( poet )

sānjiǎo ( triangle ) — shānjiǎo ( foothill )

dǎsǎn ( use umbrella ) — dǎshǎn ( lightning )

xiànzài — xiàncài ( amaranth )

nánshān — lǎnsǎn ( lazy )

gōnglǐ — gōnglì ( the Gregorian calendar )

4. Memorize the following words :

nán  běi              shān                  chē

5. Substitution drills :

A :    Kěyǐ $\begin{cases} \text{dāchē} \\ \text{jìnlái (come in)} \\ \text{zuòxia (sit down)} \\ \text{chōuyān (smoke cigarette)} \end{cases}$ ma ?

B :   Kěyǐ.

     Qǐngba.

     Kěyǐ , qǐngba.

6. Dialogue :

( 1 ) Q :

     Qǐngwèn , zhè dào $\begin{cases} \text{jīchǎng (airport)} \\ \text{dòngwùyuán (the zoo)} \\ \text{Gùgōng} \\ \text{Chángchéng} \\ \text{Zhōngguó yínháng} \\ \text{(Bank of China)} \end{cases}$ duō yuǎn?

     A : _____ gōnglǐ.

( 2 ) Q : Qǐngwèn , nǐ de chē qù nán shān ma ?

     A : Shì de , _____.

     Bú shì , _____.

7. Translate the following sentences into Chinese :

    ( 1 ) Excuse me , how far is it from here to the South Hills ? And to the North Hills ?

    ( 2 ) Could you give me a ride ?

    ( 3 ) I went to the Great Wall yesterday .

    ( 4 ) I am sorry ! —It's all right .

    ( 5 ) May I come in ? —Come in , please .

# Lesson Twelve

## Text

△ : Gēge, míngtiān dìlǐ kǎoshì, nǐ kǎokao wǒ ba.

Elder Brother, there will be a geography test tomorrow. Quiz me.

○ : Hǎo! Shāndōng zài nǎr?

All right. Where is Shandong?

△ : Shāndōng zài Zhōngguó de dōngbù.

Shandong is in the eastern part of China.

○ : Xīzàng zài nǎr?

Where is Tibet?

△ : Xīzàng zài Zhōngguó de xībù.

Tibet is in the western part of China.

○ : Hénán zài nǎr?

Where is Henan?

△ : Hénán zài Huánghé de nánbian.

Henan is south of the Yellow River.

○ : Héběi zài nǎr?

Where is Hebei?

△ : Héběi zài Huánghé de běibian.

Hebei is north of the Yellow River.

○ : Nàme, Huánghé zài nǎr?

Then, where is the Yellow River?

△ : Ńg—Nǐ shuō ne?

Mm... Where do you think?

| | | | | | |
|---|---|---|---|---|---|
| gēge | n. | elder brother | nàme | ad. | then （serving to change the tone of speech） |
| míngtiān | n. | tomorrow | | | |
| dìlǐ | n. | geography | ńg | | mm … （exclamation showing doubt） |
| dōngbù | n. | eastern part | | | |
| xībù | n. | western part | Shāndōng | | Shandong （Province） |
| nánbian | n. | southern part | | | |
| běibian | n. | northern part | Xīzàng | | Tibet |
| kǎoshì | n. | test | Hénán | | Henan （Province） |
| kǎo | v. | to test, to take an exam | Huánghé | | the Yellow River |
| zài | v. | to be at | Héběi | | Hebei （Province） |
| shuō | v. | to speak, to talk | | | |

## Explanations of the Text

1. Kǎo-kao is formed by doubling the verb kǎo. It implies that the action is a trial or of very short duration. Most monosyllabic verbs in Chinese can be used in this way. For example : shuō — shuōshuo ; kàn — kànkan ; liù — liùliu （Lesson 9）. The second syllable is toneless.

2. In Chinese, there are four main words of direction : dōng, nán, xī, běi. A direction word followed by bù means in the... part. For example : Shànghǎi zài Zhōngguó de dōngbù （Shanghai is in the eastern part of China）. A direction word followed by biān means to the.... For example : Rìběn zài Zhōngguó de dōngbiān （Japan is to the east of China）.

## Sentence Patterns

A : ✕ ✕ zài nǎr ?

B :

| Shāndōng | | | | |
|---|---|---|---|---|
| Héběi | zài | Zhōngguó | de | běibian. |
| Hénán | | Huánghé | | nánbian. |
| Xīzàng | | | | xībù. |
| | | | | dōngbù. |

# Exercises

1. Read aloud the following syllables :

| | | | | | | | |
|---|---|---|---|---|---|---|---|
| xī | dī | lī | nī | gē | dē | mē | hē |
| bā | nā | mā | dā | shān | zhōng | tiān | dōng |
| áo | láo | zuó | zhuó | hé | huáng | nán | yáng |
| běi | kǎo | wǒ | hǎo | nǐ | sǎn | shǎn | zhǎng |
| zàng | zài | shì | bù | qù | dào | jìn | jìng |

2. Tone drills :

| | | | |
|---|---|---|---|
| Shāndōng | Hénán | Huánghé | Kǎokao |
| kǎoshì | Xīzàng | dìlǐ | dōngbù |
| Zhōngguó | nàyàng | nàme | míngtiān |

3. Sound discrimination :

zài — zhài

zàng — zhàng

zǐ ( purple ) — zhǐ ( paper )

zāngzuǐ ( dirty mouth ) — zhāngzuǐ ( open the mouth )

zāihuā ( plant flowers ) — zhāihuā ( pick flowers )

4. Memorize the following words :

| | | | | |
|---|---|---|---|---|
| gēge | míngtiān | dìlǐ | kǎo | kǎoshì |
| shuō | zài | nàme | yuǎn | kěyǐ |

$$
\text{běi}
\begin{cases}
\text{bù} \\
\text{bian}
\end{cases}
$$

N

$$
\text{xī}
\begin{cases}
\text{bù} \\
\text{bian}
\end{cases}
\qquad W \qquad E \qquad
\text{dōng}
\begin{cases}
\text{bù} \\
\text{bian}
\end{cases}
$$

S

$$
\text{nán}
\begin{cases}
\text{bù} \\
\text{bian}
\end{cases}
$$

5. Fill in the blanks :

（1）Rìběn zài Zhōngguó de _____.

（2）Zhōngguó zài Měiguó de _____.

（3）Éguó zài Zhōngguó de _____.

（4）Měiguó zài Jiānádà ( Canada ) de _____.

（5）Nánjí（the South Pole）zài dìqiú（the Earth）de _____.

（6）Běijí（the North Pole）zài dìqiú de _____.

6. Dialogue：

（1）Q：Jiānádà zài nǎr？

　　A：Jiānádà zài Měiguó de _____.

（2）Q：Zhōngguó zài nǎr？

　　A：Zhōngguó zài Éguó de _____.

　　A：Zhōngguó zài Rìběn de _____.

7. Substitution drills：

Nǐ
$\left\{ \begin{array}{l} \text{kǎokao} \\ \text{jiāojiao（teach）} \\ \text{bāngbang（help）} \\ \text{kànkan} \end{array} \right\}$
wǒ ba.

8. Shuōshuo Huánghé，Zhōngguó zài nǎr？

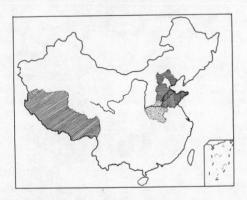 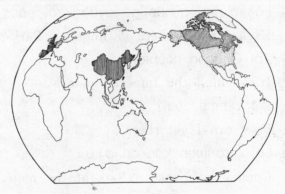

9. Translate the following sentences into Chinese：

（1）China is situated in the eastern hemisphere；the U.S.A. is situated in the western hemisphere.

（2）My friend is learning Chinese in Beijing.

（3）Little girl，what's your name？

（4）The Yellow River is to the south of the Great Wall；the Great Wall is to the north of the Yellow River.

（5）There will be a Chinese language test tomorrow. Please quiz me.

# Lesson Thirteen

**Text**

△ : Láojià , Jǐngshān gōngyuán zài nǎr ?

Excuse me , where is Jingshan Park ?

○ : Zài Gùgōng hòubian .

It's behind the Imperial palace .

△ : Wǒ zěnme zǒu ?

How can I get there ?

○ : Lái , zánmen kànkan dìtú .

Come , let's take a look at the map .

△ : Duìbuqǐ , wǒ bú rènshi Hànzì .

I'm sorry , but I can't read Chinese .

○ : Ò , nín cóng zhèr xiàng qián zǒu , xiàng zuǒ guǎi , zài xiàng yòu guǎi , jiù dào le .

Oh , I see . You go straight ahead from here , then turn left , next turn right , and there you are .

△ : Xièxie !

Thank you !

○ : Bú kèqi !

Not at all .

**Vocabulary**

| | | | | | |
|---|---|---|---|---|---|
| gōngyuán | *n.* | park | dìtú | *n.* | map |
| hòu(-bian) | *n.* | behind | Hànzì | *n.* | Chinese characters |

| | | | | | | |
|---|---|---|---|---|---|---|
| qián(-bian) | *n.* | front | | guǎi | *v.* | to turn |
| zuǒ(-bian) | *n.* | left | | kèqi | *a.* | polite, courteous |
| yòu(-bian) | *n.* | right | | cóng | *prep.* | from |
| zěnme | *ad.* | how | | xiàng | *prep.* | toward |
| zánmen | *n.* | we | | zài | *ad.* | again |
| láojià | | excuse me | | jiù | *ad.* | at once, right away |
| zǒu | *v.* | to walk, to go | | Jǐngshān | | Jingshan Park (Coal |
| lái | *v.* | to come | | gōngyuán | | Hill Park) |
| kàn(kan) | *v.* | to look at, to see | | Gùgōng | | Imperial Palace |
| rènshi | *v.* | to know, to recognize | | | | (Palace Museum) |

## Explanations of the Text

1. The difference between the pronouns zánmen and wǒmen: zánmen includes both the speaker and the person spoken to; but wǒmen does not include the person spoken to.

2. Zài is an adverb if used before a verb. For example: zài xuéxí, zài tiàowǔ. Zài is a verb if used before a noun. For example: Wǒ zài Běijīng. Tā zài Měiguó. Zài is sometimes a preposition. For example: Zài jiàoshì xuéxí, zài gōngyuán.

## Sentence Patterns

A:
Qǐngwèn / Láojià } qù { Jǐngshān gōngyuán / Gùgōng / Yíhéyuán / Chángchéng } zěnmezǒu?

B:
Nínxiàng { qián / zuǒ / yòu / dōng / nán / xī / běi } zǒu, zàixiàng { zuǒ / yòu / dōng / xī / nán / běi } guǎi, jiù dào le.

**Exercises**

1. Read aloud the following syllables :

   rī    rí    rǐ    rì

   rēn    rén    rěn    rèn

   rāng    ráng    rǎng    ràng

   Zhōngguó rén    Měiguó rén    Rìběn rén

   Wǒ wèi rén rén , rén rén wèi wǒ .

   ( I serve everyone ; everyone serves me . )

2. Tone drills :

   láojià — lǎojiā ( hometown )

   gōngyuán — gòngyuàn

   Hànzì — hànzi ( man )

   rènshi — rénshì ( the world )

   kèqi — kěqì ( exasperating )

3. Memorize the following words :

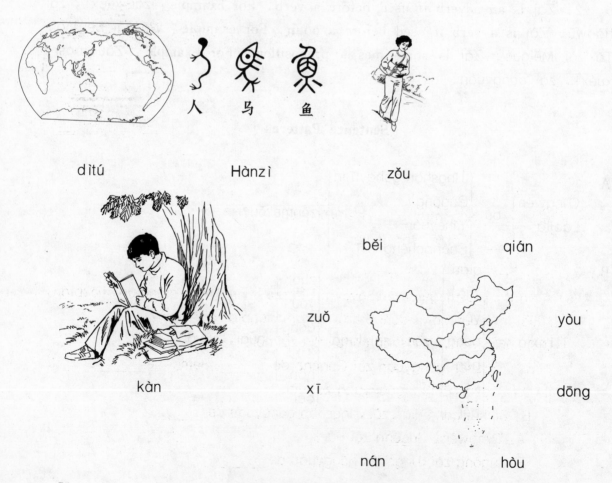

   dìtú          Hànzì          zǒu

                                běi          qián

   zuǒ                                        yòu

   kàn          xī                           dōng

                 nán                hòu

74

4. Fill in the blanks:

(1) Fill in the blanks with wǒmen or zánmen:

_____ shì Měiguó rén.          _____ shì hǎo péngyou.

(2) Fill in the blanks with cóng… xiàng…:

i) _____ Běihǎi (Beihai Park)
   _____ dōng zǒu, shì Jǐngshān.

ii) _____ Běihǎi _____ dōng zǒu, zài
    _____ nán guǎi, shì Gùgōng.

iii) _____ Gùgōng _____ běi zǒu, zài
     _____ xī guǎi, shì Běihǎi.

(3) According to the picture above, fill in the blanks with qiánbian, hòubian,
    zuǒbian, yòubian or dōngbian, xībian, nánbian, běibian:
    i) A: Qǐngwèn, Jǐngshān gōngyuán zài nǎr?
       B: Jǐngshān gōngyuán zài Gùgōng de _____, Běihǎi de _____.
    ii) A: Láojià, Běihǎi gōngyuán zài nǎr?
        B: Běihǎi gōngyuán zài Jǐngshān gōngyuán de _____.
    iii) A: Qǐngwèn, Gùgōng zài nǎr?
         B: Gùgōng zài Jǐngshān gōngyuán de _____.

75

5. Dialogue:

(1) Answer the following questions according to the picture above:

Q:
Láojià, qù ⎰Gùgōng
⎰Jǐngshān gōngyuán⎰ zěnmezǒu?
⎱Běihǎi gōngyuán

A: Nín _____.

(2) Look at the following picture: Who is supposed to say láojià, xièxie, búkèqi?

nǚ: _____! 　　　　nǚ: _____!
　　　　　　　　　　　　nán: _____!

6. Make sentences following the examples:

|  | Topic(subject) | Modifier | Declarative (predicate) |
|---|---|---|---|
| Example: | Nǐ | hěn | cōngming. |
|  | Nǐ | xiàng qián | zǒu, |
|  |  | xiàngzuǒ | guǎi. |

(1) hěn hǎo wǒ

(2) xiǎo shìjiè zhēn

(3) tiàowǔ zuótiān wǎnshang nǐ le

(4) kǎo dìlǐ míngtiān wǒ

7. Translate the following sentences into Chinese:

(1) Have you ever been to the Louvre?

(2) Excuse me, how far is it from here to the Temple of Heaven?

(3) Excuse me, where is the Imperial Palace? How can I get there?

(4) How can I get to the London Bridge from here?

(5) Where have you been? Have you been to the Great Wall (The Imperial Palace, Beihai Park and Coal Hill Park)?

# Summary (Lessons 11-13)

## Communicative Expressions

1. Commonly used direction words:

    dōng  nán  xī  běi  (bian, bù)

    qián  hòu  zuǒ  yòu  (bian, bù)

    zhōng (jiān) (middle)

    Shàng(bian) (above)   xià(bian)(below)

2. Asking directions:

    Q: Qǐngwèn⎫
       Láojià  ⎬ , × × zài ⎰nǎr?
                        ⎱shénme dìfang (place)?

    A:
                        ⎧dōng⎫
                        ⎪nán ⎪
                        ⎪xī  ⎪
                        ⎪běi ⎪
       × × zài × × de ⎨qián⎬ bian(bù).
                        ⎪hòu ⎪
                        ⎪zuǒ ⎪
                        ⎩yòu ⎭

3. Asking about one's way to a place:

    Q: Qǐngwèn⎫ ⎰qù × ×           ⎫
       Láojià  ⎬ ⎱cóng zhèr dào × ×⎬ zěnmezǒu?
    A: Nǐ cóng zhèr xiàng × × zǒu, (zài) xiàng × × guǎi, jiù dào le.

4. Asking about distance:

    Q: Qǐngwèn⎫
       Láojià  ⎬ (cóng) zhèr dào × × duō yuǎn?
    A: × × gōnglǐ.

## Grammar

1. Notional words in Chinese:

    Notional words make up the bulk of vocabulary in Chinese. They are used to indicate various things and their properties, characteristics and states, or their movement, development and change. In other languages notional words are usually divided into three categories: noun, verb and adjective. At present, teachers and researchers of Chinese in China have also, as a rule, divided notional words into these three categories. However, we should point out that some notional words in Chinese often stand for a thing in one place, but indicate a certain property, state or change in another place, without any change in form. When we make sentences with them, they can show up in different syntactic positions (subject, object, predicate or other elements). For example:

Tā hěn shòu.

Tā shòu le.

The first shòu indicates the state; the second shòu indicates a change. Another example:

Tā xuéxí Hànyǔ.

Tā de xuéxí hěn hǎo.

The first xuéxí stands for an activity, and is used as the predicate. The second xuéxí is a noun and is used as the subject. The two xuéxí are identical in form.

2. Attribute and adverbial:

Often there are modifiers before the subject and the object. They are called attributes. In the following sentences, the words in parentheses are attributes.

(Wǒ de) shēntǐ hěn hǎo.

Tā shì (wǒ de) péngyou.

Very often there are also modifying and restrictive expressions before the predicate. These are called adverbials. The words in the square brackets are adverbials:

Nǐ [hěn] cōngming.

Nǐ [xiàng qián] zǒu.

The usual syntactic order is: (attribute) subject [adverbial] predicate (attribute) object.

**Understanding China**

China is located in the eastern part of Asia, on the west coast of the Pacific O-cean. It covers an area of 9.6 million square kilometres. Administratively, the country is divided into 3 municipalities: Beijing, Tianjin and Shanghai; 23 provinces, including Hebei, Henan, Shandong, Shanxi, Hainan and Taiwan; and 5 autonomous regions; Tibet, Xinjiang, Inner Mongolia, Ningxia and Guangxi. Under the provinces and autonomous regions there are cities and counties.

China has a total population of 1.1 billion which consists of 56 nationalities including Han, Tibetan, Mongolian, and Hui.

The two great rivers in China are the Yangtse River and the Yellow River, which are the two cradles of civilization of China.

As one of the oldest civilizations in the world, China has a recorded history of 5,000 years. The country's capital is Beijing.

The Great Wall is one of the most famous ancient architecture structures in the world. It starts from the Bohai Sea in the east and ends at Jiayuguan Pass, Gansu Province in the west, extending 7,300 kilometres. It stands as a witness to the long history of the Chinese nation and a symbol of the wisdom and strength of the Chinese people.

## Humour

1. Máquè (sparrow) hé (and) yànzi (swallow)

Lǎoshī: "Zhè shì niǎo (bird), nà yě shì niǎo. Qǐng (please) tóngxuémen (pupils) shuōshuo, nǎ shì yànzi, nǎ shì máquè?"

Tóngxué (pupil): "Máquè pángbiān (beside) shì yànzi, yànzi pángbiān shì máquè."

2. Zài nǎr dǎzhēn (have injection)

Hùshi (nurse) gěi (preposition introducing object) bìngrén (patient) dǎzhēn. Hùshi wèn: "Nín shuō, zài nǎr dǎzhēn hǎo?" Bìngrén shuō: "Nǐ wèn wǒ ma?" "Shì a!" "Nà (then) jiù zài nǐ de gēbo (arm) shàng (on) dǎ (give—here give the injection) ba."

3. Shénme shíhou (time) qǐchuáng (get up)

"Nǐ měitiān (everyday) shénme shíhou qǐchuáng?" "Tàiyáng (the sun) gāng ( ad. just) zhàodào (shine on) wǒ de chuānghu (window), wǒ jiù qǐchuáng le."

"Nǐ qǐchuáng hěn zǎo a!"

"Bù zǎo, wǒ de chuānghu cháo (v. to face) xī ya (an auxiliary word)!"

## Introduction to Chinese Characters

One of the limitations of a picture language is that abstract ideas can not be expressed by pictures or images. Therefore, ancient Chinese created some new methods. One of them was to combine two or more pictures to express a more complicated idea. For example:

| | | | |
|---|---|---|---|
| 休 | 休 | xiū | The left part means a man, and the right part is a tree. A man is leaning against a tree having a rest. |
| 林 | 林 | lín | Trees standing side by side—woods. |
| 森 | 森 | sēn | Here are more trees growing luxuriantly. It is a big forest. |
| 東 | 东 | dōng | The sun rises to about half a tree's height. It suggests the direction from which the sun rises. |
| 北 | 北 | běi | Two men are standing back to back. It means back. Geographically, China is situated in the northern temperate zone. The houses usually face south. Therefore, the back of the houses face north. |
| 西 | 西 | xī | The pictograph looks like a bird and a nest. When the sun sets in the west, birds return to their nests. |
| 看 | 看 | kàn | The upper part is a hand and the lower part is an eye. When you place your hand above your eyes, you are looking at something in the distance. |
| 好 | 好 | hǎo | The left part is a woman, and the right part is a child. Put together, they come to mean a young woman, which therefore carries the meaning of good and beautiful. |
| 明 | 明 | míng | The sun and moon together mean brightness. |

# Lesson Fourteen

**Text**

△: Nǐ qù guo Běijīng fàndiàn ma?

Have you ever been to Beijing Hotel?

○: Jīngcháng qù.

I go there often.

△: Nàr de cài zěnmeyàng?

How is the food there?

○: Hěn hǎochī.

It's very delicious.

△: Shénme cài zuì hǎochī?

What is the best dish there?

○: Kǎoyā zuì hǎochī.

The best is roast duck.

△: Hái yǒu ne?

Anything else?

○: Jiǎozi yě búcuò.

Dumplings are also very good.

△: Nà zánmen xiànzài jiù qù ba.

Then let's go there now.

○: Ê—xiànzài bùxíng.

Well—not now.

△: Wèishénme?

Why?

◯: Qián zài wǒ àiren nàr ne.

My wife has got the money.

## Vocabulary

| | | | | | | |
|---|---|---|---|---|---|---|
| fàndiàn | n. | hotel，restaurant | nà | | | |
| kǎoyā | n. | roast duck | hǎochī | a. | delicious | |
| jiǎozi | n. | dumplings | búcuò | a. | not bad，good | |
| qián | n. | money | bùxíng | | won't do，be out of | |
| àiren | n. | wife or husband de-pending on the situa-tion | | | the question | |
| | | | yǒu | v. | to have | |
| nàr(nà+er) | ad. | there | jīngcháng | ad. | often | |
| zěnmeyàng | | how about，what about | zuì | ad. | most | |
| | | | ê | | an auxiliary word showing hesitation | |
| wèishénme | ad. | why | | | | |

## Explanations of the Text

1. Zuìhǎo，hěnhǎo，hǎo，búcuò stand respectively for the different degrees of hǎo. Chinese very often uses adverbs to differentiate the various degrees of an adjective.

2. The auxiliary word ne has two main usages. At the end of an interrogative sentence，a higher pitch should be used. For example：Hái yǒu ne? At the end of a declarative sentence，a lower pitch should be used. For example：Qián zài wǒ àirén nàr ne. Please note that the ne in this second sentence implies a state of continuation，namely：my wife still has the money.

## Sentence Patterns

Shénme $\left\{ \begin{array}{l} \text{(bù)} \\ \text{(zuì)} \end{array} \right\}$ hǎochī?

Jiǎozi
Kǎoyā
Zhōngguó cài $\left\{ \begin{array}{l} \text{(bù)} \\ \text{(zuì)} \end{array} \right\}$ hǎochī.
Rìběn cài
Měiguó cài

82

## Exercises

1. Read aloud the following syllables：

| | | |
|---|---|---|
| jīng | qīng | xīng |
| jù | qù | xù |
| jiǎo | qiǎo | xiǎo |
| jiù | qiú | xiù |
| jiào | qián | xiàn |

2. Tone drills：

| | | | |
|---|---|---|---|
| bēi | (béi) | běi | bèi |
| jīng | (jíng) | jǐng | jìng |
| fān | fán | fǎn | fàn |
| diān | (dián) | diǎn | diàn |
| chāng | cháng | chǎng | chàng |
| jiāo | jiáo | jiǎo | jiào |
| kāo | (káo) | kǎo | kào |
| zāi | (zái) | zǎi | zài |
| qiān | qián | qiǎn | qiàn |
| xiān | xián | xiǎn | xiàn |
| xīng | xíng | xǐng | xìng |

3. Tone discrimination：

Běijīng—bèijǐng (background)

jīngcháng—jìngchǎng (clear the cinema or theatre of all watchers at the end of
the show)

jiǎozi—jiàozi (sedan chair)

hǎochī—hàochī (be gluttonous，love to eat)

àiren—ǎirén (dwarf)

bùxíng—búxìng (unfortunate)

4. Memorize the following words：

(1)

| Běijīng | fàndiàn | kǎoyā |
|---|---|---|

jiǎozi                qián

(2) àiren      yǒu     hǎochī     búcuò

bùxíng     zuì     jīngcháng

zěnmeyàng      wèishénme

5. Substitution drills：

(1) Q：

Nǐ qù guo { Běijīng fàndiàn / Gùgōng / Chángchéng / Zhōngguó / Rìběn } ma?

A：Wǒ qù guo.（or：Wǒ jīngcháng qù.）

(2) Q： Nàr de cài / Zhōngguó cài / Fǎguó cài / Diànshì jiémù（TV programme）/ Nǐ de shēntǐ } zěnmeyàng?

A：

Nàr de cài { hěn hǎo. / tǐng hǎo de. / búcuò. / hái còuhe. / mǎmahūhū. }

6. Dialogue：

(1) Q：Nǐ de qián zài nǎr?

A：Wǒ de qián zài _____.

(2) Q：Nǐ de shū zài zhèr ma?

A：Wǒ de shū bú zài zhèr，zài _____.

(3) Q：Nǐ bàba zài nǎli?

A：Wǒ bàba zài _____.

7. Translate the following sentences into Chinese：

(1) Have you ever been to Beijing Hotel?

(2) I often have Chinese food.

(3) Peking Duck is really delicious.

(4) How do you like the television programmes?

(5) Let's go to the Great Wall now.

# Lesson Fifteen

**Text**

△: Nǐ kàn, wǒ shòu le ma?

Do you think I've lost weight?

○: Wǒ kànkan, méi zěnme shòu, hǎoxiàng pàng le.

Let me see. Not really. You seem to have put on weight.

△: Zěnme huì ne? Wǒ zhèng jiǎnféi ne.

How come? I've been trying to lose weight.

○: Nǐ zěnme jiǎn?

In what way?

△: Měi tiān wǎnfàn jiǎn yíbàn.

I'm eating only half as much at dinner.

○: Nǐ de juéxīn hěn dà.

You really are determined.

※　　※　　※

□: Liǎng wèi xiānsheng, yào diǎn shénme?

Excuse me, sir. What would you like?

○: Wǒ yào yí fèn niúpái, yì bēi píjiǔ.

I'd like beefsteak and a glass of beer.

□: Xiānsheng, nín ne?

And you, sir?

△: Wǒ yào liǎng fèn niúpái, liǎng píng píjiǔ.

I'd like to have two beefsteak and two bottles of beer.

○: Ǎ?

What?

## Vocabulary

| | | | | | | |
|---|---|---|---|---|---|---|
| tiān | *n.* | day | jiǎn | *v.* | to reduce, to lose |
| wǎnfàn | *n.* | dinner, supper | yào | *v.* | to want, to desire |
| yíbàn | *n.* | half | liǎng | *n. a.* two |
| juéxīn | *n.* | determination | yī | *n. a.* one |
| niúpái | *n.* | beefsteak | wèi | *mea.* (used for person) |
| píjiǔ | *n.* | beer | diǎn | a bit |
| měi | *a.* | every | bēi | a glass of |
| pàng | *a.* | fat, stout | fèn | a portion of |
| dà | *a.* | big, large | píng | a bottle of |
| méi | *ad.* | no, not | hǎoxiàng | *v.* to seem |
| huì | *v.* | can | zhèng | *ad.* in the process of, in the course of |
| jiǎnféi | *v.* | to lose weight | | | |

## Explanations of the Text

1. Measure words indicate the unit of things and actions. Those that indicate the unit of things are called noun measure words. In Chinese, appropriate noun measure words are required between a numeral and a noun. For example: 2 wèi xiānsheng, 1 fèn niúpái, 1 bēi píjiǔ, 2 píng píjiǔ.

2. A very limited number of monosyllabic words in Chinese have tonal changes in actual speech. For example: the numeral yī is pronounced as yī when it is pronounced by itself or when it is placed at the end of a word, a sentence or a string of numerals. For example: shíyī, dà xiǎo bù yī (of big and small sizes). When it is placed before a 4th-tone syllable, it changes to the 2nd tone. For example: yíbàn, yífèn. When placed before the 1st, 2nd and 3rd tones, it changes to the 4th tone. For example: yì bēi píjiǔ, yì píng píjiǔ, yìqǐ (together) qù Chángchéng.

## Sentence Patterns

$$
\text{Wǒ zhèng} \left\{ \begin{array}{l} \text{jiǎnféi} \\ \text{kǎoshì} \\ \text{xuéxí} \\ \text{diào yú} \\ \text{kàn diànshì} \end{array} \right\} \text{ne.}
$$

## Exercises

1. Read aloud the following syllables:

   shōu       shóu       shǒu       shòu

   pāng       páng       pǎng       pàng

   xiāng      xiáng      xiǎng      xiàng

   jiān       (jián)     jiǎn       jiàn

   juē        jué        juě        juè

   xīn        xín        (xǐn)      xìn

   xiān       xián       xiǎn       xiàn

   pīng       píng       pǐng       pìng

2. Tone drills:

   (1) Tonal changes of the third tone and toneless syllables:

   zěnme      hǎoxiàng      jiǎnféi

   píjiǔ      kànkan        xiānsheng

   (2) Read aloud the ne in the following sentences and explain their different functions:

   Zěnme huì ne?

   Wǒ zhèng jiǎnféi ne.

   (3) Read aloud the number yi in the following expressions, paying attention to its tonal changes in different combinations:

   yī     shíyī     tǒngyī

   bù guǎn sān qī èr shí yī

   yì jiā rén        yì bēi jiǔ        yì zhī yān

   yì píng cù        yì tiáo yú        yì tóu niú

   yì wǎn miàn       yì shǒu shī       yì kǒu zhū

   yí jiàn shì       yí yàng cài       yí jù huà

3. Sound discrimination:

   kàn—gàn (to do)       kànkan—gàngan

xiànzài—xiàncài       juéxīn—juéxǐng（to wake up）

pàngzi（a fat person）—bàngzi（club, stick）

dùzi bǎo le（the stomach is full）—tùzi pǎo le（the rabbit has run away）

4. Memorize the following words：

（1）

pàng              shòu              niúpái

píjiǔ              bēi              píng

（2）wǎnfàn     juéxīn     jiǎnféi

hǎoxiàng     liǎngwèi     yífèn

5. Fill in the blanks with appropriate measure words：

1 _____ chá              1 _____ píjiǔ

1 _____ niúpái          2 _____ kěkǒukělè （Coca Cola）

2 _____ lǎoshī          2 _____ xiānsheng

6. Substitution drills：

Q：Nǐ yào diǎn shénme?

A：

Wǒ yào {
　yì bēi kāfēi.
　yì píng（bēi）píjiǔ.
　yí fèn niúpái.
　yí fèn Zhōngguó cài.
　（yí fèn）jiǎozi.
}

7. Dialogue：

Q：Nǐ kàn, wǒ shòu le ma?

Possible answers：

Nǐ shòu le.

Nǐ hǎoxiàng shòu le.

Nǐ méi zěnme shòu, hǎoxiàng pàng le.

If the question is:

Nǐ kàn, wǒ pàng le ma?

What are the possible answers?

_____.

_____.

_____.

8. Translate the following sentences into Chinese:

(1) I'd like to have a roast duck and two bottles of beer.

(2) Do you think he has put on weight?

(3) Mr. Li has not put on weight, but seems to have lost weight.

(4) Your husband/wife seems to have lost some weight.

(5) We are learning Chinese now.

# Lesson Sixteen

## Text

△: Jīntiān fā gōngzī, zánmen qù Běijīng fàndiàn, zěnmeyàng?

Today is pay day. Let's go to Beijing Hotel, OK?

○: Hǎo! Yìqǐ qù.

All right. Let's go together.

△: Wǒ dì-yī cì chī Zhōngguó cài.

This is the first time I've eaten Chinese food.

○: Zhè shì kuàizi.

These are chopsticks.

△: Ò! Yǒuyìsi. Hái yǒu liǎng ge bēizi.

Oh, how interesting! There are also two cups.

○: Dà bēizi hē chá, xiǎo bēizi hē jiǔ.

The large one is for tea and the small one is for liquor.

※　　※　　※

□: Liǎng wèi xiānsheng yào shénme?

What would you two gentlemen like to have?

○: Yào liǎng fèn jiǎozi, yì zhī kǎoyā.

Two servings of dumplings and one roast duck.

□: Hēshénme?

Anything to drink?

○: Liǎng bēi Máotái jiǔ. Yígòng duōshǎo qián?

Two cups of Maotai. How much will that be altogether?

□: Yígòng bā shí èr kuài wǔ máo.

Eighty-two yuan and fifty fen.

○: Wǒ fù qián.

Let me pay it.

△: Bù, bù, wǒ shì dānshēn, méiyǒu "qì-guǎn-yán", wǒ qǐngkè.

No, no. I'm not married. I haven't got a bossy wife. It's my treat.


## Vocabulary

| | | | | | | |
|---|---|---|---|---|---|---|
| jīntiān | n. | today | dìyī | a. | first, No. 1 |
| gōngzī | n. | salary, wage | bā | a. n. | eight |
| kuàizi | n. | chopsticks | shí | a. n. | ten |
| bēizi | n. | cup, glass | èr | a. n. | two |
| jiǔ | n. | liquor, wine | wǔ | a. n. | five |
| dānshēn | n. | single person | cì | n. | time |
| qìguǎnyán | n. | bronchitis (pun for "wife exercising strict control") | gè | mea. | (widely used for things; toneless in actual speech) |
| duōshǎo | | how many, how much | zhī | mea. | (uesd for animals, etc.) |
| yǒuyìsi | a. | interesting | kuài (yuán) | | yuan (Renminbi) |
| fā | v. | to hand out | máo (jiǎo) | | ten fen (Renminbi) |
| fù | v. | to pay | yìqǐ | | together |
| méiyǒu | v. | to have not | yígòng | adv. | altogether |
| qǐngkè | v. | to foot the bill, to treat | Máotái (jiǔ) | | a famous liquor in China |


## Explanations of the Text

1. The verb yǒu has two usages. One indicates possession. For example:

Wǒ yǒu yí gè gēge.

Tā yǒu yì píng Máotái jiǔ.

In this type of sentence there is usually a subject before yǒu.

The second indicates existence. For example:

(Nàr) yǒu liǎng zhī máquè.

(Zhèr) yǒu liǎng gè bēizi.

This type of sentence may use direction words as subjects. Very often they do not have subjects.

2. The measure word gè is used very extensively. It can be used with people and various things. For example:

yí gè háizi, yí gè gēge, yí gè nánrén (man)

yí gè bēizi, yí gè jīdàn (egg)

yí gè píngguǒ (apple)

The measure word zhī is mainly used with birds. For example: yì zhī máquè, yì zhī yànzi, yì zhī yā (duck).

Cì is a verbal measure word indicating the number and frequency of actions. For example: Chī yí cì Zhōngguó cài, kàn yí cì diànshì, qù yí cì xuéxiào.

3. Qìguǎnyán is a homophone of qī(wife) guǎn (control) yán (strict). In Chinese, there are many homophones and semi-homophones. The Chinese people like to take advantage of this feature to make jokes or play on words. It has also been exploited in poetry-making for rhetorical effect.

## Sentence Patterns

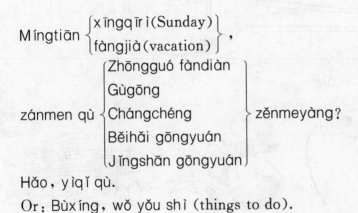

Míngtiān {xīngqīrì(Sunday) / fàngjià(vacation)},

zánmen qù {Zhōngguó fàndiàn / Gùgōng / Chángchéng / Běihǎi gōngyuán / Jǐngshān gōngyuán} zěnmeyàng?

Hǎo, yìqǐ qù.

Or: Bùxíng, wǒ yǒu shì (things to do).

## Exercises

1. Read aloud the following syllables:

| gōng | (góng) | gǒng | gòng |
|---|---|---|---|
| zī | (zí) | zǐ | zì |
| fān | fán | fǎn | fàn |
| diān | (dián) | diǎn | diàn |
| (kuāi) | (kuái) | kuǎi | kuài |
| kāo | (káo) | kǎo | kào |

kuài+er—kuàir (a lump)

tiān+er—tiānr (weather)

jīn+er—jīnr (today)

míng+er—míngr (tomorrow)

2. Read aloud the following words paying attention to the tone of yi：

   jīntiān    jīntian    yìsī    yìsi

   zánmen    zěnmeyàng    yǒuyìsi

   yígòng    yìqǐ    dìyīcì    yì zhī kǎoyā

3. Tone discrimination：

   gōngzī—gōngzǐ(son of feudal prince or high official)

   Zhōngguó—zhòng guǒ (to plant fruit)

   qìguǎn(trachea) yán(inflammation)—qī (wife) guǎn yán (strict)

   càidān (menu)—cǎidàn (coloured egg)

4. Memorize the following words：

   (1)

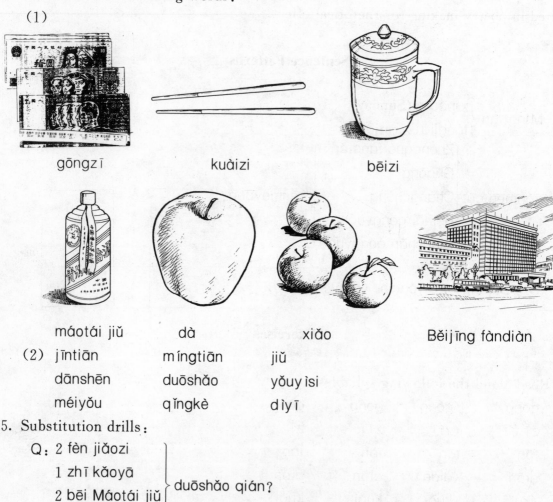

   gōngzī                kuàizi                bēizi

   máotái jiǔ        dà              xiǎo              Běijīng fàndiàn

   (2) jīntiān        míngtiān        jiǔ

       dānshēn        duōshǎo        yǒuyìsi

       méiyǒu        qǐngkè        dìyī

5. Substitution drills：

   Q：2 fèn jiǎozi

       1 zhī kǎoyā

       2 bēi Máotái jiǔ  } duōshǎo qián?

       Yígòng

A：2 fèn jiǎozi 22(èr shí èr) kuài (yuán) 5 (wǔ) máo (jiǎo) qián.

1 zhī kǎoyā 40(sì shí) kuài (yuán) qián.

2 bēi máotái jiǔ 20(èr shí) kuài (yuán) qián.

Yígòng 82 (bā shí èr) kuài (yuán) 5 (wǔ) máo (jiǎo) qián.

6. Dialogue：

Q：Nín yào shénme?

A：Wǒ yào _____.

Q：Hái yào shénme?

A：Hái yào _____.

Q：Hē shénme?

A：Hē _____.

7. Translate the following sentences into Chinese：

(1) When do we get our pay?

(2) Let's go to the Sheraton Hotel today. It's my treat.

(3) I have had dumplings in Beijing.

(4) Roast duck is really delicious. I have had roast duck at Beijing Hotel.

(5) I have never had any Maotai. What about you?

(6) Tomorrow is Sunday. Where shall we go together?

# Summary (lessons 14-16)

## Communicative Expressions

1. Asking about needs:

   Q: Nín yào diǎnr shénme?

   A: Wǒ yào yì zhī kǎoyā.

   Q: Hái yào shénme?

   A: Hái yào yí fèn jiǎozi.

   Q: Hē shénme?

   A: Yì bēi píjiǔ.

2. Asking about prices:

   Q: Yí fèn jiǎozi, duōshǎo qián?

   A: 7 (qī) kuài 5 (wǔ).

   Q: Yì bēi píjiǔ duōshǎo qián?

   A: 2 (liǎng) kuài qián.

   Q: Yígòng duōshǎo qián?

   A: Yígòng 9 (jiǔ) kuài 5 (wǔ) máo qián.

Note:

Yuán is a denomination of the Chinese currency, Renminbi. In everyday speech, people like to use kuài instead of yuán. One tenth of yuán is called jiǎo, which is often replaced by máo in everyday speech. One tenth of jiǎo is called fēn. When counting money, the unit at the end is often dropped. For example: instead of saying 1 kuài 5 máo, people only say 1 kuài 5; instead of saying 1 kuài 5 máo 5 fēn, people say 1 kuài 5 máo 5.

3. Numbers:

(1) How to read cardinal numbers:

1(yī) 2(èr) 3(sān) 4(sì) 5(wǔ) 6(liù) 7(qī) 8(bā) 9(jiǔ) 10(shí)
11(shíyī) 12(shí'èr) ······ 19(shíjiǔ) 20(èrshí) 21(èrshíyī) ······ 29(èrshíjiǔ)
30(sānshí) 31(sānshíyī) ······ 39(sānshíjiǔ) 100(yìbǎi) 101(yìbǎilíngyī)
111(yìbǎiyīshíyī) 1000(yìqiān) 10000(yíwàn) 100000(shíwàn) ······100000000
(yíyì, yí wànwàn)

Note:

In numbers that have three or more digits, the zeros that appear in the middle are pronounced líng.

(2) How to read ordinal numbers:

An ordinal number is constructed by simply putting a dì before a cardinal number. For example:

dì 1    dì 2    dì 3    dì 4  ····· dì 10

(3) Years and other numbers and codes:

1789 (yī qī bā jiǔ) nián (year)

1992 (yī jiǔ jiǔ èr) nián

14 lóu (building)  3 dānyuán (entrance of a building) 303 (sān líng sān) hào
(number).

Telephone number: 842,2244 (bá sì èr, èr èr sì sì)—3001 (sān líng líng yāo)

Note:

The 1 in telephone numbers is often pronounced as yāo so as not to be confused
with 7.

(4) The difference between èr and liǎng:

Èr is used when it is read as a numeral. For example:

1,2,3,4,···,12, dì 2,1992.

Liǎng is used when it is placed before a measure word. For example:

liǎng wèi xiānsheng    liǎng píng píjiǔ

liǎng fèn jiǎozi    liǎng bēi kāfēi

Note:

Before bǎi(hundred), qiān (thousand), wàn (ten thousand) and yì (hundred
million), liǎng is usually used. But èr is also possible. For example:

liǎng bǎi, èr bǎi;    liǎngwàn, èrwàn;

liǎng yì liǎng qiān wàn, èr yì èr qiān wàn.

## Grammar

1. A brief summary of pronouns:

| Personal Pronouns | Demonstrative Pronouns | Interrogative Pronouns |
| --- | --- | --- |
| wǒ | zhè | shuí |
| nǐ | zhèr | nǎ |
| tā | zhèli | nǎr |
| nín | zhège (this) | nǎli |
| | zhèyàng (this way) | nǎge (which) |
| wǒmen | nà | shénme |
| nǐmen | nàr | zěnme |
| tāmen | nàli (there) | zěnmeyàng |
| zánmen | nàge (that) | |
| | nàyàng | |

Note:

The interrogative pronoun is an important part of an interrogative sentence. It is often placed after the verb or the judgment word (shì). Very seldom is it placed before them or at the beginning of a sentence. This is a major difference between Chinese and many other languages. For example:

Tā shì shuí?

Nǐ xìng shénme?

Nǐ shì nǎ guó rén?

Gùgōng zài nǎr?

2. Measure words(mea.):

Measure words are a special group of words in Chinese used to indicate the unit of things and actions.

Those indicating the unit of things are noun measure words. They are placed between a numeral and a noun. For example:

1 gè rén, 44 gè shìzì, 1 wèi lǎoshī,

2 (liǎng) fèn jiǎozi, 1 zhī kǎoyā,

1 píng píjiǔ, 2 (liǎng) bēi Máotái jiǔ.

Those indicating the unit of actions are verbal measure words. They are usually placed after the verb. For example:

kàn 1 cì diànshì, chī 1 cì kǎoyā.

There are a great number of measure words in Chinese. Different nouns and verbs require different measure words. You will be learning many more measure words in future.

## Understanding China

Eating habits and communication

1. When several Chinese go to a restaurant, each expresses his or her willingness to pay the bill. Only on rare occasions do they "go dutch". A traditional idea in China is that friendship is more important than money.

2. When a Chinese entertains guests, he or she usually prepares a lot of delicious dishes, but will still say to the guests: "I haven't prepared any good dishes" or "these are just a few simple home-made dishes". What he or she actually wants to convey is that the dishes are far from enough to show his or her hospitality.

3. While eating, the host, who is eagerly attentive, will try to pick up food and put it on the guests' plate. He or she also tries to persuade the guests to drink (alcoholic drinks) from time to time. China has a long tradition of wine drinking. Both

the literati and the warriors advocated drinking. This influence is still felt today.

4. In China, people like to give nice-sounding names to various dishes. For example: bā bǎo fàn (eight-treasure rice), sì xǐ wánzi (meatballs of four happinesses), and sù shí jǐn(assorted vegetarian dish). Homonyms are often used to give symbolic meanings to dishes. For example: niánnián yǒu yú (to have surplus every year; yú is the homonym for fish), jí qìng yǒu yú (to be lucky and have surplus; jí is a homonym for chicken and yú for fish).

**Humour**

1. Míyǔ (riddle)

A riddle implies a thing through descriptions, figures, symbols and homonyms. The implied thing is called mídǐ, and the means by which something is implied is called mímiàn. For example:
Shàngbian máo (hair), xiàbian máo, zhōngjiān yí lì (a grain) hēi (black) pútao (grape).
This riddle uses description. The answer is yǎnjīng, an eye.

2. Píngguǒ shì tián (sweet) de

Zhuōzi (table) shang de píngguǒ bú jiàn (disappear) le. Māma wèn: "Shuí ná (take away) le?" Méirén shuōhuà (speak). Māma shuō: "Nà píngguǒ shì suān(sour) de, bù néng chī." Dìdi shuō: "Bù, māma, nà píngguǒ shì tián de."

3. Méi fǎ(way) chī

Lǎo Lǐ(Old Li) zài shítáng (cafeteria) chī fàn(meal), tā yào le yígè cài, fúwùyuán(waiter, waitress) duān(carry…in hand) lái cài, Lǎo Lǐ kànkan cài, shuō: "Zhè cài bù néng chī." Fúwùyuán yòu duān lái yí gè cài, Lǎo Lǐ hái shuō "bù néng chī". Fúwùyuán shuō: "Zhè cài hěn hǎo chī, nín chángchang (to taste)." Lǎo Lǐ shuō: "Bú shì cài bù hǎochī, shì méiyǒu kuàizi!"

**Introduction to Chinese Characters**

Another way the ancient Chinese created characters was by combining a symbol indicating a general category of meaning with a phonetic symbol. This was a major step forward, since it introduced for the first time a sound factor into the Chinese written language, making it more powerful in terms of expression. Meanwhile, the symbols indicating meaning can differentiate homonyms, making it possible for characters sharing similar concepts, or for semantically connected characters, to become calligraphically related. This has facilitated memory and understanding. For example:

张 zhāng：　弓 was originally written as 弜 which looks like a bow. 长 is pronounced as zhǎng, providing a similar sound. The character means to stretch a bow. Now it means to open as in "open the mouth". It is also used as a surname.

吃 chī 喝 hē：　口 is the meaning symbol, for eating and drinking must be done by mouth. 乞 is pronounced as qǐ; 曷 is pronounced as hé. They stand for the pronunciation of the two characters.

晚 wǎn 饭 fàn：　日 stands for the sun. It shows that time has to do with the revolution of the sun. 免 is pronounced as miǎn, providing a similar sound. 饣 is the simplified version of 食, meaning food. 反 is pronounced as fǎn, representing a similar sound.

烤 kǎo 鸭 yā：　火 is the meaning symbol: to burn with fire. 考 is pronounced kǎo, representing the pronunciation. 鸟 indicates that it is a kind of bird. 甲 is pronounced as jiǎ, providing a similar sound.

啤 pí 酒 jiǔ：　Both 口 and 氵 are meaning symbols. 氵 was originally written as 巛 representing water. 卑 is pronounced as bēi and 酉 is pronounced as yǒu, providing similar sounds.

钱 qián：　钅 is the simplified version of the radical 金 (jīn); it is the meaning symbol representing money. 戋 is pronounced as jiān, providing a similar sound.

芳 fāng：　The upper part of the character was originally written as 屮屮. This is the meaning symbol, representing flowers and grass. The lower part is the sound symbol, pronounced as fāng, representing the pronunciation. This character means the fragrant smell of flowers and grass. It is often used in female names.

菜 cài：　艹 is the meaning symbol, showing that it is related to plants and vegetables. 采 is pronounced as cǎi, representing a similar sound.

筷 kuài 子 zi：　⺮, originally written as 竹竹, is the meaning symbol. It stands for bamboo. From ancient times chopsticks have often been made of bamboo. 快 is pronounced as kuài, representing the sound.

请 qǐng 客 kè：　讠 is the simplified version of the radical 言. It is the meaning symbol representing language. 青 is pronounced qīng, providing a similar sound. 宀 originally written as 穴, is the meaning symbol. It stands for house or roof. 各 is pronounced as gè representing a similar sound.

# Lesson Seventeen

**Text**

Shǐmìsī: (qiāo mén) Do, do, do.

(Knocking on the door) Knock, knock.

Wáng: Qǐng jìn! Ā! Shǐmìsī xiānsheng, Shǐmìsī fūren, huānyíng guānglín!

Come in! Ah! Mr. and Mrs. Smith. Welcome!

Shǐmìsī: Wáng xiānsheng, gěi nín bàinián!

Mr. Wang, Happy New Year!

Wáng: Bùgǎndāng, bùgǎndāng! Wǒ jièshào yíxià: Zhè shì wǒ àiren, zhè shì wǒ dà érzi, érxífù.

It's very kind of you. Let me introduce (to you, this is) my wife, (this is) my eldest son, (this is) my daughter-in-law.

Shǐmìsī: Nǐmen hǎo!

How do you do!

Wáng: Zhè shì wǒ de lǎoèr.

This is my second son.

Lǎo'èr: Wǒ jiào Wáng Xiǎopéng, jīnnián 15 suì.

My name is Wang Xiaopeng. Fifteen years old this year.

Shǐmìsī: Nǐ hǎo! Liǎng dài rén, 5 kǒu zhī jiā, zhēn shì xìngfú de jiātíng.

How do you do! You are a happy family indeed, five members, two generations.

Lǎo'èr: Hái yǒu tā—yì zhī māo—ne, tā jiào Wáng Xiǎomī.

And there is one more—a cat. His name is Wang Xiaomi.

Shǐmìsī： Ò, duì, duì! Hái yǒu tā. Wáng Xiǎomī, nǐ jǐ suì le?

Oh, sure! He must be included. Wang Xiaomi, how old are you?

Lǎo'èr： Tā liǎng suì le.

He is two.

## Vocabulary

| | | |
|---|---|---|
| mén | *n.* | door |
| érzi | *n.* | son |
| érxífù | *n.* | daughter-in-law |
| jīnnián | | this year |
| suì | *n.* | age |
| jiā | *n.* | family, home |
| jiātíng | *n.* | family |
| māo | *n.* | cat |
| jǐ | | how many, several |
| xìngfú | *a.* | happy |
| qiāo | *v.* | knock |
| qǐng | | please |
| jìn | *v.* | come in, go in |
| guānglín | *v.* | to be present at a place (a courteous way to refer to someone's visit to the speaker's home or a function he hosts) |
| bàinián | *v.* | to wish somebody a Happy New Year |
| bùgǎndāng | | I really don't deserve this; you flatter me. |
| jièshào | *v.* | to introduce |
| xià | *mea.* | (used for actions) |
| dài | *n.* | generation |
| kǒu | *mea.* | (used for people) |
| gěi | *prep.* | (introducing the object of action) |
| dō | | an onomatope, sound of knocking |
| ā | | exclamation showing surprise |
| lǎo | | prefix showing the order of children, very much like dì |
| zhī | | auxiliary word connecting noun with noun; it resembles de in function |

## Explanations of the Text

1. The communicative expressions in this lesson—xiānsheng, fūren, guānglín and bùgǎndāng —are elegant expressions used on formal occasions. The auxiliary zhī is an expression handed down from ancient Chinese. It is refined, but is not frequently used in daily speech.

2. Dà is often used to mean the eldest child among siblings. For example: dà gē, dà jiě and dà érzi. Lǎo is used to differentiate the age order among siblings and

children. For example: lǎo dà, láo èr and lǎo sān.

## Sentence Patterns

1.
Wǒ gěi $\left\{\begin{array}{l}\text{nǐ}\\ \text{nín}\\ \text{tā}\end{array}\right\}$ $\left\{\begin{array}{l}\text{bàinián.}\\ \text{xiě xìn (write letter).}\\ \text{dǎ diànhuà (telephone).}\\ \text{jiǎng gùshi (tell a story).}\end{array}\right.$

2. Wǒ (lái) jièshào yí xià, zhè (wèi) shì···.

## Exercises

1. Read aloud the following syllables:

| qiāo | qiáo | qiǎo | qiào |
| guāng | (guáng) | guǎng | guàng |
| (līn) | lín | lǐn | lìn |
| bāi | bái | bǎi | bài |
| niān | nián | niǎn | niàn |
| gān | (gán) | gǎn | gàn |
| dāng | (dáng) | dǎng | dàng |
| lǎo èr | liǎng suì | liǎng dài rén | |

2. Tone drills:

xiānsheng　　fūren　　àiren　　nǐmen　　hǎo

érxífù　　1 zhī māo　　1 kǒu rén　　1 gè jiātíng

3. Tone and sound discrimination:

qiāo mén—qiào mén(to prize open a door)

bàinián—bǎinián(one hundred years)

xífù(son's wife)—xīfú(western suit)

xìngfú—xìnfú(to be convinced)

4. Memorize the following words:

(1)

qiāo　　　　　　mén　　　　　　jìn

|  | bàinián | jièshào | érzi érxífù | māo |
|---|---|---|---|---|
| (2) | jīnnián | jiā | jiātíng | huānyíng |
|  | guānglín | suì | xìngfú | qǐng |
|  | bùgǎndāng | jǐ | dài | kǒu |

5. Substitution drills:

Wǒ (lái) jièshào yíxià, zhè(wèi)shì
{
Wáng xiānsheng.
Wáng tàitai(Mrs.).
Lǎo Wáng.
Xiǎo Lǐ.
Zhāng lǎoshī.
wǒ de péngyou Lǎo Lǐ.
}

6. Dialogue:

—Gěi nǐ (nín)
{
bàinián!
dào chá(to pour tea).
jìng jiǔ(to propose a toast).
}
—Bùgǎndāng, bùgǎndāng!

—Gěi nín bàinián!
　　　(dào chá)
　　　(jìng jiǔ)
—Xièxie!

7. Translate the following sentences into Chinese：
   (1) Mr. and Mrs. Smith wish Mr. Wang a Happy New Year.
   (2) Mr. Wang said：Welcome!
   (3) There are five people in Mr. Wang's family：they are Mr. Wang and his wife, his two sons and a daughter-in-law.
   (4) Wang Xiaopeng is fifteen this year.
   (5) There is a cat in Mr. Wang's home.
   (6) Let me introduce：this is Mr. Johnson, a good friend of mine.

# Lesson Eighteen

## Text

Shǐmìsī fūren: Wáng xiānsheng, nín yě zuò fàn?

Mr. Wang, you also cook?

Wáng: Píngshí wǒ àiren zuò fàn, jīntiān máng, wǒ dǎda xiàshǒu.

Usually my wife does the cooking. Since she's busy today, I'm just helping.

Shǐmìsī fūren: Rénmen dōu shuō: yīnggāi jià Zhōngguó zhàngfu, qǔ Rìběn tàitai, zhè huà búcuò.

I heard that one should marry a Chinese husband or take a Japanese wife. That's well said.

Wáng tàitai: Nín hái kuā tā? Píngshí lǎn zhene.

You speak too highly of him. Usually he is very lazy.

Shǐmìsī: Cài tài fēngshèng le.

What a feast!

Wáng: Jiācháng fàn cài, bù chéng jìngyì!

Just some simple homely dishes, quite inappropriate for entertaining guests.

Shǐmìsī fūren: Hěn hǎochī, wèidao hǎo jí le.

Very delicious! They taste extremely good!

Shǐmìsī: Zhù nǐmen quán jiā xìngfú, gānbēi!

A toast to the happiness and health of your family!

Wáng: Zhào Zhōngguó xíguàn, zánmen gān wán zhè bēi.

Let's finish the whole glass (of liquor) according to Chinese custom.

Shǐmìsī: Bùxíng, bùxíng, nín shì hǎiliàng, wǒ gān bài xià fēng!

I'm sorry I can't. You can drink a lot. I'm no match.

## Vocabulary

| | | | | | | |
|---|---|---|---|---|---|---|
| fàn | *n.* | food | qǔ | *v.* | (of a man)to marry |
| píngshí | | usually | kuā | *v.* | to praise |
| xiàshǒu | *n.* | help | zhù | *v.* | to wish |
| rénmen | *n.* | people | gānbēi | *v.* | to drink the whole cup of liquor, bottoms up |
| zhàngfu | *n.* | husband | | | |
| tàitai | *n.* | Mrs. | | | |
| huà | *n.* | speech, saying | gān | *v.* | to dry |
| wèidao | *n.* | taste, flavour | wán | *v.* | to finish |
| xíguàn | *n.* | custom, habit | dōu | *ad.* | all |
| hǎiliàng | *n.* | great capacity for liquor | tài | *ad.* | too |
| | | | jí | *ad.* | extremely |
| máng | *a.* | busy | zhào | *prep.* | according to |
| lǎn | *a.* | lazy | zhene | | an auxiliary word showing a great extent or degree |
| fēngshèng | *a.* | sumptuous, great variety of··· | | | |
| jiācháng | *a.* | homely | bù chéng | | This is not enough to show my respect for you. |
| quán | *a.* | whole, complete | jìngyì | | |
| zuò | *v.* | to do, to make | | | |
| dǎ | | here it means to do or to make | gān bài | | I am no match. |
| | | | xià fēng | | |
| yīnggāi | | should | dǎ xiàshǒ | | to give some help |
| jià | *v.* | (of a woman) to marry | | | |

## Explanations of the Text

1. The predicate (verb or adjective) is often followed by adverbs or other verbs, in order to show extent or result. For example:

Wèidao hǎo jí le.

Zánmen gān <u>wán</u> zhè bēi.

This is a unique syntactic structure in Chinese. You will come across similar structures in future.

2. The adverb bù also has tonal changes in oral speech. The rule of thumb is: it is in the 4th tone when it is used by itself or before characters of the 1st, 2nd and 3rd tones: bù, bù hē, bù xíng, bù hǎo. But before a 4th-tone character, it changes to the 2nd tone: bú cuò, bú jiàn and búshì.

## Sentence Patterns

1. Wèidao hǎo jí le.

Cài $\begin{Bmatrix} \text{hǎochī} \\ \text{fēngshèng} \end{Bmatrix}$ jíle.

2. Zánmen $\begin{Bmatrix} \text{gān} \\ \text{chī} \\ \text{hē} \end{Bmatrix}$ wán $\begin{Bmatrix} \text{zhè bēi.} \\ \text{zhè zhī kǎoyā.} \\ \text{zhè píng píjiǔ.} \end{Bmatrix}$

## Exercises

1. Read aloud the following syllables:

| | | | |
|---|---|---|---|
| yīng | yíng | yǐng | yìng |
| gāi | (gái) | gǎi | gài |
| (lān) | lán | lǎn | làn |
| fēng | féng | fěng | fèng |
| shēng | shéng | shěng | shèng |
| jīng | (jíng) | jǐng | jìng |

2. Tone drills:

| | | | |
|---|---|---|---|
| búcuò | búduì | búqù | búhuì |
| bùchī | bùhē | bùxiāng | bùduō |
| bùxíng | bùchéng | bùpíng | bùtián |
| bùhǎo | bùzǎo | bùlǎo | bùshǎo |

3. Sound discrimination:

ü—i

qǔ—qǐ (to get up)

xié (shoe)—xué

xiě—xuě (snow)

qù—qì (machine)

4. Memorize the following words:

    zuò     fàn     máng    lǎn    zhàngfu

    tàitai    fēngshèng    xìngfú    xíguàn

    hǎiliàng    jiācháng    quánjiā    gānbēi

    píngshí    yīnggāi    wèidao    rénmen

    dǎ xiàshǒu    bù chéng    jìngyì    gān bài xià fēng

5. Substitution drills:

Wáng xiānsheng $\begin{Bmatrix} \text{lǎn} \\ \text{máng} \\ \text{pàng} \\ \text{shòu} \end{Bmatrix}$ zhene!

Cài $\begin{Bmatrix} \text{hǎo} \\ \text{duō} \\ \text{hǎochī} \\ \text{fēngshèng} \end{Bmatrix}$ zhene!

6. Fill in the blanks with jí and wán:

    (1) Wáng xiānsheng lǎn _____ le.

    (2) Wáng xiānsheng máng _____ le.

    (3) Wáng xiānsheng de jiātíng xìngfú _____ le.

    (4) Shǐmìsī hē _____ jiǔle.

    (5) Wǒ chī _____ kǎoyā le.

    (6) Tā kàn _____ diànshì le.

7. Dialogue:

    (1) Q: Píngshí Wáng xiānsheng zuòfàn ma?

        A: _____.

    (2) Q: Rénmen dōu shuō: "Yīnggāi jià Zhōngguó zhàngfu, qǔ Rìběn tàitai."

           Zhè huà duì ma?

        A: _____.

8. Translate the following sentences into Chinese:

    (1) There are five people in Mr. Wang's family. There is also a cat.

    (2) Mr. Wang's family is extremely happy.

    (3) Mr. Wang is usually very busy.

    (4) Mrs. Smith likes Chinese food very much; her husband likes Maotai.

    (5) They all say: Chinese food is extremely delicious!

    (6) Mr. Wang has drunk a cup of Maotai.

# Lesson Nineteen

**Text**

Shǐmìsī fūren: Jīntiān zhēn gāoxìng!

We are very happy today!

Wáng tàitai: Zhāodai bù zhōudao, qǐng yuánliàng!

Please forgive us for not entertaining you well.

Shǐmìsī fūren: Nǎli, yànhuì hěn fēngfù, zhǔren yòu hěn rèqíng, wǒmen hěn yúkuài.

Just the opposite. The dinner is sumptuous; our host is warm-hearted. We are very happy.

Shǐmìsī: Chī le Sìchuān cài, yòu hē le Máotái jiǔ, jiǔ zú fàn bǎo, gāi gàocí le.

We have had Sichuan dishes and Maotai. We have had enough wine and food and been well entertained, and we must say good-bye now.

Wáng tàitai: Wǒmen sòng yí sòng.

We'll see you off.

Shǐmìsī fūren: Búyòng sòng, nín qǐng huí.

Please don't bother to come any further.

Wáng xiānsheng: Nín màn zǒu, huānyíng zài lái.

(You) take care. Welcome to come again.

Shǐmìsī: Gǎnxiè nín de zhāodài, qǐng liúbù.

Thank you for your hospitality. Please don't bother to come any further.

110

| Lǎo'èr: | Shūshu, āyí, zàijiàn! |
| | Uncle and Aunt, good-bye! |
| Shǐmìsī: | Xiǎopéng, zàijiàn! Xiǎomī, zàijiàn! |
| | Good-bye, Xiaopeng! Good-bye, Xiaomi! |

## Vocabulary

| | | | | | | |
|---|---|---|---|---|---|---|
| yànhuì | n. | banquet, dinner | zhāodài | v. | to treat, to entertain |
| zhǔren | n. | host | yuánliàng | v. | to forgive, to excuse |
| zhāodài | n. | hospitality | gāi | | should |
| shūshu | n. | uncle | gàocí | v. | to say good-bye |
| āyí | n. | aunt | sòng | v. | to see off |
| nǎli | | a courteous expression of negation | búyòng | | don't need to |
| | | | huí | v. | to return, to go back |
| gāoxìng | a. | happy | | | |
| zhōudao | a. | thoughtful | gǎnxiè | v. | to thank |
| fēngfù | a. | sumptuous, a great variety of | liúbù | v. | to stay behind, to stop going further |
| rèqíng | a. | warm-hearted | jiǔ zú fàn bǎo | | a Chinese idiom: to |
| yúkuài | a. | pleased | | | have plenty of food |
| zú | a. | enough | | | and wine |
| bǎo | a. | full | Sìchuān | | a province in south- |
| màn | a. | slow | | | western China |

## Explanations of the Text

1. Gàocí, liúbù and jiǔzúfànbǎo are somewhat elegant expressions and idioms often used on formal occasions.

2. Sòng yí sòng is a usage similar to the doubling up of a verb. Any doubled verb can have a yí inserted between the two characters. For example:

liùliù—liù yí liù,     kànkan—kàn yí kàn.

3. In this text we have come across the second type of usage of the character le: chī le Sìchuān cài, hē le Máotái jiǔ.

In previous lessons le always showed up at the end of a sentence. It is used mainly to express an affirmative mood and often indicates that something has happened or a change has taken place. In its second type of usage le is placed right after the verb to show that the action is finished. Apart from the examples in the lesson, we can also say: Lǎo Wáng kàn le diànshì, dìdi kǎo le dìlǐ, and Shǐmìsī jiàn le Wáng xiānsheng.

## Sentence Patterns

1. Gǎnxiè nǐ de $\begin{cases} zhāodāi. \\ bāngzhù\ (help). \\ lǐwù\ (gift). \end{cases}$

   Possible answers:

   Búyòng xiè(thank)!

   Bú kèqi!

2. Yànhuì hěn fēngfù, zhǔren yòu hěn rèqíng.

   There are similar patterns. For example:

   Tā hěn cōngming, xuéxí yòu hěn nǔlì (hard).

   Tā hěn pàng, wǎnfàn yòu chī liǎng fèn niúpái.

## Exercises

1. Read aloud the following syllables:

   | | | | |
   |---|---|---|---|
   | yuān | yuán | yuǎn | yuàn |
   | xuān | xuán | xuǎn | xuàn |
   | wō | (wó) | wǒ | wò |
   | duō | duó | duǒ | duò |
   | yū | yú | yǔ | yù |
   | jū | jú | jǔ | jù |
   | yī | yí | yǐ | yì |
   | dī | dí | dǐ | dì |
   | wān | wán | wǎn | wàn |
   | duān | (duán) | duǎn | duàn |

2. Tone drills:

   bùgǎndāng    bú kèqi    búcuò    bùxíng

   bù chéng jìngyì    bù zhōudao    búyòng sòng

   jièshào yíxià    yìzhī māo    sòng yí sòng

3. Sound discrimination:

   u-ü

   yú-wú            yuán — wán

112

|  |  |  |  |  |
|---|---|---|---|---|
| lùdēng | (street lamp) | — | lǜdēng | (green light) |
| lùdì | (land) | — | lǜdì | (lawn) |
| lúzi | (stove) | — | lǘzi | (donkey) |

4. Memorize the following words:

yànhuì    zhǔren    rèqíng    zhāodài    jiǔ zú fàn bǎo    yúkuài

gǎnxiè    gàocí    liúbù    sòng    huí    zài lái    yuánliàng

gāoxìng    zhōudao    fēngfù    gāi    yīnggāi    búyòng    màn zǒu

5. Dialogue:

After dinner the guest may say to the host:

(1) _____.

(2) _____.

The guest has said good-bye and come out of the house. The host should say:

(1) _____.

(2) _____.

The guest asks the host not to see him/her off:

(1) _____.

(2) _____.

6. Make complete sentences by combining two short phrases using the adverb yòu:

(1) chī Zhōngguó cài, hē Zhōngguó jiǔ

(2) xuéxí Hànyǔ, xuéxí Yīngyǔ

(3) kǎo dìlǐ, kǎo Hànyǔ

(4) shàngbān, guǎn háizi

7. Translate the following sentences into Chinese:

(1) Mr. and Mrs. Wang are from Sichuan.

(2) The host is warm and thoughtful.

(3) Mrs. Smith says Sichuan food is extremely delicious.

(4) Mr. Smith loves Maotai best.

(5) Mr. and Mrs. Smith are very pleased.

(6) Today, the dinner is sumptuous and we are warmly treated. We are so happy!

# Summary (lessons 17-19)

## Communicative Expressions

1. Asking about age:

    Q: Xiǎo péngyou, nǐ jǐ suì?

       How old are you, little friend?

    A: Jīnnián 8 suì.

       I'm eight this year.

    Q: Xiǎo Lǐ, nǐ duō dà le?

       How old are you, Xiao Li?

    A: 22 le.

       I'm twenty-two.

    Q: Wáng shīfu, nín duō dà niánjì?

       Mr. Wang, how old are you?

    A: Jīnnián 58 le.

       I'm fifty-eight this year.

    Q: Lǎodàye (grandpa), nín jīnnián gāoshòu (your venerable age)?

       Grandpa, how old are you (what's your venerable age) this year?

    A: Wǒ? 76 le.

       Me? Seventy-six.

Note:

The Chinese have different ways of asking about the age of people of different age groups. When asking about the age of a middle-aged or old person, they use polite expressions.

2. Expressions of introduction:

    Wǒ(lái) jièshào yí xià, zhè(wèi) shì…

3. New year greeting and toasting expressions:

    (1) Gěi nín bàinián!

       Xīnnián (New Year) hǎo!

       Xīnnián kuàilè(happy)!

    (2) Zhù nín $\begin{cases} \text{xìngfú} \\ \text{jiànkāng (healthy)} \end{cases}$, gānbēi!

Note:

This way of making a toast is identical with international practice. You may take one sip and not finish the whole glass.

Zánmen gān wán zhè bēi!

Zánmen gān!

Note:

This is China's traditional way of toasting. Both persons must finish the whole glass and then turn the glass upside down or sideways (facing the opening of the glass to the other person) to show that the glass is empty.

4. Parting expressions:

Jiǔ zú fàn bǎo, gāi gàocí le.

Wǒ gàocí le.

Wǒ sòng yí sòng.

Nín màn zǒu, huānyíng zài lái.

Búyòng sòng, nín qǐng huí.

Qǐng liúbù.

## Grammar

A brief summary of parts of speech in Chinese

1. Notional words:

Notional words denote things and their properties, characteristics and changes. They include the following items:

(1) Nouns. For example:

Zhōngguó jiātíng rén xiānsheng fūren cài chá kāfēi kǎoyā jiǎozi

Attached to these words are:

(a) Direction words. For example:

dōng nán xī běi shàng xià zuǒ yòu páng (side) zhōng (centre)

Direction words can be follwoed by biān, bù, jiān, miàn.

(b) Time words. For example:

jīntiān jīnnián míngtiān zǎoshang wǎnshang

(2) Verbs. For example: zǒu xuéxí kàn chī hē qǐng zhāodài.

There are a few verbs that indicate relationship and existence.

For example: shì yǒu zài

Attached to verbs are auxiliary verbs. For example: néng gāi huì.

(3) Adjectives. For example: dà xiǎo cōngming hǎochī hǎo pàng shòu xìngfú fēngfù fēngshèng.

The nouns, verbs and adjectives mentioned above constitute the notional words in Chinese.

115

(4) Pronouns (words replacing notional words). For example:

nǐ wǒ tā zhè nà nǎ shuí shénme zěnme

(5) Numerals and measure words. For example:

yī èr sān sì … shí bǎi qiān wàn yì

dìyī dì'èr dì sān

gè wèi zhī bēi píng fèn

2. Words of relationship:

These are words indicating the relationship between notional words. They include the following items:

(1) Prepositions (words introducing nouns and pronouns to verbs, and indicating time, place, object and manner). For example: cóng xiàng zài zhào.

(2) Conjunctions (words connecting different words, phrases and sentences). For example: hé gēn (with) tóng (together)

(3) Structure words (words combining notional words with their modifiers and complements). For example: de (de$_1$, de$_2$, de$_3$ have the same pronunciation and spelling but they are used in different structures.)

3. Auxiliary words:

These words help describe certain additional meanings of notional words. They include the following items:

(1) Adverbs (words indicating the extent, time, manner, affirmation and negation of verbs and adjectives). For example: bù hěn zhēn tài jí jīngcháng.

Some adverbs serve as words of relationship, combining word groups and sentences. For example: yòu … yòu … .

(2) Tense words (words that help describe the tense and form of verbs). For example: le guo zhe.

(3) Auxiliary words indicating mood(used at the end of sentences). For example: le ma ne ba de.

4. Isolated words:

These are words that cannot be combined with any other words. The major form is in exclamations, words used to express such emotions as surprise, doubt and interjection. For example: ā ǎo ò.

## The Chinese Family

Chinese people attach great importance to the family. So far, life without a family is still considered abnormal. Relations in a Chinese family are generally stable, as

116

people in China believe that there should be harmony and intimacy between members of a family. Those who do not live with their parents often visit them during the holidays, and many pensioners live with their children. In the old days, people talked highly of extended families with four or five generations living under one roof. Nowadays, the size of the family has become smaller, mostly having three to four members today. At home, husbands share in household chores, a practice seen as a modern virtue.

Commonly Used Appellations of Relations for Five Generations

| Generation | Type of Relative | How to Call |
|---|---|---|
| 1st generation | (paternal)<br>grandfather<br>grandmother | yéye<br>nǎinai |
| | (maternal)<br>grandfather<br>grandmother | lǎoye<br>lǎolao |
| 2nd generation | father<br>mother | bàba<br>māma |
| | wife's<br>father<br>mother | yuèfù<br>yuèmǔ |
| | husband's<br>father<br>mother | gōnggong<br>pópo |
| | father's<br>elder brother<br>his wife | bóbo<br>bómu |
| | father's<br>younger brother<br>his wife | shūshu<br>shěnshen |
| | father's<br>sister<br>her husband | gūmā<br>gūfù |
| | mother's<br>brother<br>his wife | jiùjiu<br>jiùmā |
| | mother's<br>sister<br>her husband | yímā<br>yífù |

| Generation | Type of Relative | How to Call |
|---|---|---|
| 3rd generation | husband | àiren, xiānsheng |
| | wife | àiren, tàitai |
| | elder brother | gēge |
| | his wife | sǎosao |
| | elder sister | jiějie |
| | her husband | jiěfū |
| | younger brother | dìdi |
| | his wife | dìmèi |
| | younger sister | mèimei |
| | her husband | mèifū |
| | father's brother's children | |
| | elder brother | tángxiōng |
| | elder sister | tángjiě |
| | younger brother | tángdì |
| | younger sister | tángmèi |
| | children of father's sister and mother's brothers and sisters | |
| | elder brother | biǎogē |
| | elder sister | biǎojiě |
| | younger brother | biǎodì |
| | younger sister | biǎomèi |
| 4th generation | son | érzi |
| | his wife | érxífù |
| | daughter | nǚér |
| | her husband | nǚxù |
| 5th generation | son's children | |
| | grandson, his wife | sūnzi, sūnxífù |
| | granddaughter, her husband | sūnnǚ, sūn nǚxù |
| | daughter's children | |
| | daughter's son, his wife | wàisun, wàisun xífù |
| | daughter's daughter, her husband | wàisunnǚ wàisun nǚxù |

**Humour**

1. Bàba, érzi hé sūnzi (grandson)

Xǔ Jìngzōng (name of a person) shì gǔdài (ancient times) yí gè dà guān (official). Tā de érzi Xǔ Áng (name of a person) zhǐ zuò le xiǎo guān. Xǔ Áng de érzi Xǔ Yànbó (name of a person) hěn niánqīng (young) jiù hěn yǒu míngqi (fame). Yì tiān, Xǔ Jìngzōng duì (to) Xǔ Áng shuō: "Wǒ de érzi bùrú (not as good as) nǐ de érzi." Xǔ Áng mǎshàng (at once) huídá (answer): "Tā de bàba bùrú wǒ de bàba."

118

2. Míyǔ

Yí yàng (kind) dōngxi (thing) bú pà (be afraid of) gōnggong (father-in-law) pà pópo (mother-in-law).

There is something that is not afraid of gonggong but popu.

Tā shì làzhú (candle).

Note:

Pópo are aspirated sounds. A candle will be blown out if you say pópo.

3. Family relations in *A Dream of Red Mansions*

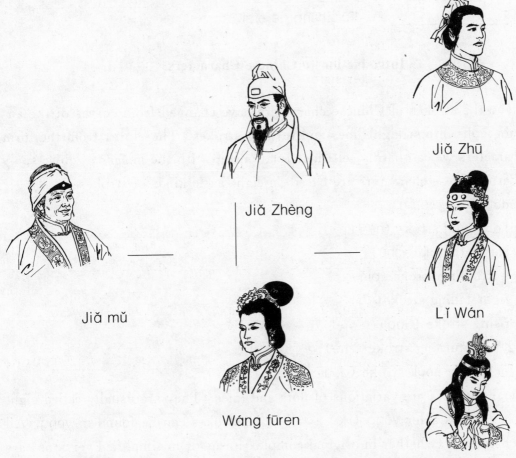

Jiǎ Zhū

Jiǎ Zhèng

Jiǎ mǔ

Lǐ Wán

Wáng fūren

Jiǎ Bǎoyù

*A Dream of Red Mansions* is a famous classical Chinese novel. Since it was made into a film and a TV serial in the 1980s, the characters and plot have become known to almost everyone in China. It has been regarded as an encyclopaedia of the feudal Chinese lifestyle.

First you will be introduced to the relationships of a group of people in the novel. Then fill in the blanks.

Jiǎ Zhèng shì Jiǎ mǔ (mother) de érzi, Wáng fūren shì Jiǎ Zhèng de àiren, Jiǎ Zhū shì Jiǎ Zhèng de dà érzi, Jiǎ Bǎoyù shì Jiǎ Zhèng de lǎo èr, Lǐ Wán shì Jiǎ

Zhū de àiren.

    (1) Jiǎ mǔ shì Jiǎ Zhèng de _____.

    (2) Jiǎ Bǎoyù shì Jiǎ mǔ de _____.

    (3) Jiǎ Zhèng shì Jiǎ Bǎoyù de _____.

    (4) Wáng fūren shì Jiǎ mǔ de _____.

    (5) Lǐ Wán shì Jiǎ mǔ de _____.

    (6) Lǐ Wán shì Wáng fūren de _____.

    (7) Jiǎ Zhū shì Jiǎ Bǎoyù de _____.

    (8) _____ hé _____ shì Jiǎ Zhèng de érzi.

## Introduction to Chinese Characters

Today，the strokes of Chinese characters have changed from curves of the ancient pictographs into straight lines and turning strokes. Therefore，from the form of the characters we can hardly tell their relationship with the images of objects.

Modern Chinese characters are based on eight basic kinds of strokes：

" 、 "——dot stroke (diǎn)

" 一 "——horizontal stroke (héng)

" 丨 "——vertical stroke (shù)

" 丿 "——left-falling stroke (piě)

" 乀 "——right-falling stroke (nà)

" ㇀ "——rising stroke (tiǎo)

" 乚 , 𠃌 , 乙 "——turning stroke (zhé)

" 刁 , 宀 , 弋 , 乚 "——hook stroke (gōu)

All eight strokes are variations of dots and lines. They are usually called eight methods of the character yǒng （永） as all eight strokes can be found in yǒng. All Chinese characters (whether in original complex forms or in simplified versions) are composed of these eight basic strokes. The characters formed by the combination of these strokes turn out to be square in shape. So Chinese characters are also called square characters.

As far as writing is concerned，there are a few basic rules：

1. From top to bottom：

    一 二 (èr)

    丨 上 上 (shàng)

    丶 宀 宀 字 字 字 (zì)

    一 一 一 西 西 要 要 要 要 (yào)

120

2. From left to right：

丿 人 (rén)

丿 川 川 (chuān)

丶 丷 氵 汈 汉 (hàn)

丨 叮 叮 叫 叫 (jiào)

3. From outside to inside：

丨 冂 冃 日 (rì)

丨 冂 叼 四 四 (sì)

丨 冂 冋 回 回 回 (huí)

丨 冂 冂 冋 冎 国 国 国 (guó)

You can write almost all the Chinese characters by following these rules：

丿 亻 伫 仵 佇 你 你 (nǐ)

乀 女 女 奼 好 好 (hǎo)

丿 入 亼 今 (jīn)

一 二 于 天 (tiān)

一 十 去 击 赱 幸 幸 幸 (xìng)

丶 亅 礻 礻 祁 祒 祒 祒 祒 福 福 福 福 (fú)

# Lesson Twenty

## Text

Mǎlì: Chūnjié kuài dào le.

It'll soon be Spring Festival (Chinese New Year).

Tāngmǔ: Jīntiān shì jǐ hào?

What's the date today?

Mǎlì: Jīntiān shì 2 yuè 17 hào. Míngtiān shì chúxī, hòutiān shì Chūnjié.

Today is the 17th of February. Tomorrow is New Year's Eve, and the day after tomorrow is New Year's Day.

Tāngmǔ: Chúxī zhènghǎo shì xīngqī 6, tài hǎo le.

New Year's Eve falls on a Saturday. Wonderful!

Mǎlì: Xiǎo Wáng, zánmen zhǔnbèi yí xià ba?

Xiao Wang, let's make some preparations.

Xiǎo Wáng: Hǎo, wǒ xiě duìlián, nǐmen zhǔnbèi niánfàn.

All right. I'll write the couplets and you prepare the food.

Mǎlì: Zánmen dōu chuān Zhōngguó yīfu ba. Wǒ yǒu yí tào zhìfú hé yì dǐng jiěfàng mào.

Let's put on Chinese clothes. I have a Chinese suit and a Chinese army cap.

Xiǎo Wáng: Zhè zhǒng yīfu zài 80 niándài jiù bù liúxíng le.

Those clothes were outdated even in the 80's.

Tāngmǔ: Kàn wǒ zhège.

Look at mine.

Mǎlì：　Hā！Guāpímào hé mǎguà，zhēn hǎowánr！

Ha！A skullcap and a mandarin jacket. They are so funny！

Tāngmǔ：　Zuótiān wǒ cóng Zhōnghuá jiē mǎi lái de. Hǎo ma？

I bought them on Zhonghua Street yesterday. Aren't they nice？

Xiǎo Wáng：Zhège ma—chuān shàng jiù chéng chūtǔ wénwù le.

Well，you'd become an unearthed cultural relic if you wear them.

## Vocabulary

| | | | | | |
|---|---|---|---|---|---|
| Chūnjié | *n.* | Chinese New Year，Spring Festival | zhǔnbèi | *v.* | to prepare |
| hào | *n.* | date | xiě | *v.* | to write |
| yuè | *n.* | month | chuān | *v.* | to put on |
| chúxī | *n.* | New Year's Eve | jiěfàng | *v.* | to liberate |
| hòutiān | *n.* | the day after tomorrow | liúxíng | *v.* | to be in fashion |
| xīngqī | *n.* | week | mǎi | *v.* | to buy |
| duìlián | *n.* | couplet | shàng | *v.* | up |
| niánfàn | *n.* | food for New Year's Day | chéng | *v.* | to become |
| yīfu | *n.* | clothes | chūtǔ | *v.* | to unearth |
| zhìfú | *n.* | suit，uniform | tào | *mea.* | set |
| mào | *n.* | hat，cap | dǐng | *mea.* | (used for hat) |
| niándài | *n.* | year | zhǒng | *mea.* | kind |
| guāpímào | *n.* | skullcap | kuài | *ad.* | fast |
| mǎguà | *n.* | mandarin jacket | zhènghǎo | *ad.* | just，exact |
| jiē | *n.* | street | hé | *conj.* | and |
| wénwù | *n.* | cultural relic | hā | | an exclamation |
| zhège | | pronoun，this | ma | | a modal auxiliary word |
| hǎowánr | *a.* | funny，interesting | Zhōnghuá | | China，often name of people or places |

## Explanations of the Text

1. The verbs lái and shàng in mǎi lái and chuān shàng are used after another verb to describe，as a complement，the result of the action. We came across this type of usage in Lesson Eighteen. These are just two more

123

examples. We called these elements complements.

The yí xià in zhǔnbèi yí xià is a measure word used after the verb. It is also a complement, indicating the verb's quantitative unit.

2. The number qī and bā in 2 yuè 17 hào and 80 niándài may also have tonal changes in actual speech. In short, before characters of the 1st, 2nd and 3rd tones, they should take the 1st tone; but before a 4th-tone character they should change to the 2nd tone. For example:

| | | | |
|---|---|---|---|
| dì qī | dì bā | qī zhī | bā bēi |
| qī shí | bā shí | qī píng | bā píng |
| qī zhǒng | bā dǐng | qī fèn | bá wèi |

## Sentence Patterns

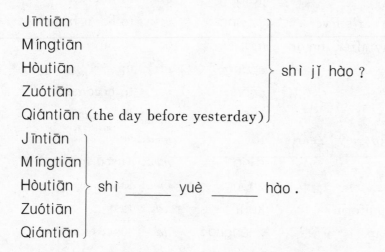

## Exercises

1. Read aloud the following syllables:

| | | | | |
|---|---|---|---|---|
| jīn+er | — | jīnr | míng+er | — míngr |
| hòu+er | — | hòur | mào+er | — màor |
| yíkuài+er | — | yíkuàir | duìlián+er | — duìliánr |
| mǎguà+er | — | mǎguàr | hǎowán+er | — hǎowánr |

2. Tone drills (paying attention to the tone of qi and ba):

dì 7    27    98    38

7 bēi    8 gēn    7 yuán    8 máo

7 wǎn    8 liǎng    7 wèi    8 kuài

3. Tone discrimination:

chúxī — chūxi (promising)
Chūnjié — chúnjié (pure)
yīfu — yífu (uncle)
xīngqī — xíngqī (prison term)
liúxíng — liúxīng (meteor)

4. Memorize the following words :

( 1 )

duìlián          yīfu              zhìfú           jiěfàng mào

guāpímào        mǎguà            jiē            chūtǔ wénwù

( 2 ) xīngqī    niándài        zhǔnbèi      liúxíng

zhènghǎo       chuān        xiě      mǎi      chéng

hòutiān       zhège        yuè      hé      dào

niánfàn       chúxī        Chūnjié

5. Substitution drills :

( 1 ) A :    Jīntiān
             Míngtiān
             Hòutiān     shì xīngqī jǐ?
             Zuótiān
             Qiántiān

      B :                        rì(Sunday).
             Jīntiān             1.
             Míngtiān            2.
             Hòutiān    shì xīngqī  3.
             Zuótiān             4.
             Qiántiān            5.
                                 6.

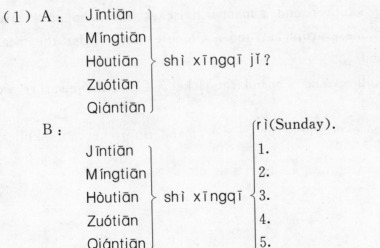

（2）　　　Guāpímào
　　　　　Wáng Xiǎomī
　　　　　Xióngmāo（panda）　} zhēn hǎowánr！
　　　　　Zhège xiǎo gūniang

6．Fill in the blanks：

　　（1）Jīntiān shì 8 yuè 1 hào．
　　　　Míngtiān shì ＿＿＿＿ yuè ＿＿＿＿ hào．
　　　　Hòutiān shì ＿＿＿＿ yuè ＿＿＿＿ hào．
　　　　Zuótián shì ＿＿＿＿ yuè ＿＿＿＿ hào．
　　　　Qiántiān shì ＿＿＿＿ yuè ＿＿＿＿ hào．
　　（2）Jīntiān shì xīngqī 1．
　　　　Míngtiān shì xīngqī ＿＿＿＿．
　　　　Hòutiān shì xīngqī ＿＿＿＿．
　　　　Zuótiān shì xīngqī ＿＿＿＿．
　　　　Qiántiān shì xīngqī ＿＿＿＿．

7．Talking about dates and months of the calendar：

　　（1）In Chinese the names of the months are very simple．They are formed by adding yuè to the numerals 1 to 12．Now say the 12 months in Chinese．

　　（2）In Chinese，besides Sunday，which is called xīngqīrì or xīngqītiān，the names of the other 6 days are made up of xīngqī and numbers from 1 to 6．Now say the 7 days in Chinese．

8．Translate the following sentences into Chinese：

　　（1）It will soon be New Year's Eve．It is on the 18th of February．

　　（2）February 19th is Spring Festival．

　　（3）Tom bought a skullcap and a mandarin jacket from Zhonghua Street．

　　（4）Mary has a Chinese army hat and a Chinese suit．（Use the measure words dǐng and tào．）

　　（5）Tom has a skullcap and a mandarin jacket．（Use the measure words dǐng and jiàn．）

　　（6）Now the Chinese people wear neither mandarin jacket nor skullcaps．

# Lesson Twenty-one

## Text

| | |
|---|---|
| Tāngmǔ | Xiǎo Wáng, Chūnjié hǎo! |
| Mǎlì | Xiao Wang, Happy Spring Festival! |
| Xiǎo Wáng: | Gōngxǐ, gōngxǐ, dàjiā Chūnjié hǎo! |
| | Congratulations! Happy Spring Festival to you! |
| Mǎlì: | Wǒ sòng nǐ yì zhāng hèniánkǎ. |
| | Here is a new year greeting card for you. |
| Xiǎo Wáng: | Zhēn piàoliang! Xièxie! |
| | It's so pretty! Thanks! |
| Tāngmǔ: | Wǒ sòng nǐ yì píng Máotái jiǔ. |
| | Here is a bottle of Maotai for you. |
| Xiǎo Wáng: | Hǎo xiāng a! Fēicháng gǎnxiè. |
| | It really smells good. Thank you very much! |
| Mǎlì: | Zhè fù duìlián zěnme niàn? Shì shénme yìsi? |
| | How do you read this couplet? What does it mean? |
| Xiǎo Wáng: | Zhè fù duìlián zhèyàng niàn: "Yì yuán fù shǐ, wàn xiàng gēng xīn." |
| | Yìsi shì: xīn de yì nián kāishǐ le, gè zhǒng dōngxi dōu yǒu le xīn de shēngmìng. |
| | This couplet reads: Yì yuán fù shǐ, wàn xiàng gēngxīn. It means the new year has begun; every thing has a new life. |
| Tāngmǔ: | Kèren dào qí le ma? |
| | Are all the guests here? |

Xiǎo Wáng ： Hái chà yí wèi, shì Jiānádà tóngxué.

Everyone is here except one—a student from Canada.

Mǎlì ： Zánmen xiànzài bāo jiǎozi ba.

Let's start making dumplings.

Tāngmǔ ： Chī wán niánfàn zánmen kāi yí gè wǎnhuì, tòngtongkuàikuài de wánr yí gè wǎnshang.

After the meal let's have a party and enjoy the evening.

## Vocabulary

| | | | | | | |
|---|---|---|---|---|---|---|
| hèniánkǎ | n. | new year greeting card | xīn | a. | new |
| yìsi | n. | meaning | qí | a. | all present |
| nián | n. | year | tòngkuai | a. | to one's heart's content |
| dōngxi | n. | thing | | | |
| shēngmìng | n. | life | gōngxǐ | v. | to congratulate |
| kèren | n. | guest | sòng | v. | to present |
| tóngxué | n. | fellow student | niàn | v. | to read |
| wǎnhuì | n. | party | kāishǐ | v. | to begin |
| dàjiā | n. | everyone | chà | v. | to lack |
| zhèyàng | n. | this kind | bāo | v. | to wrap up |
| gè | a. | various | kāi | v. | to hold (a party or meeting) |
| piàoliang | a. | pretty, beautiful | | | |
| xiāng | a. | fragrant (nice smell) | wánr | v. | to play, to have a good time |
| fēicháng | ad. | very | | | |
| de | | a word connecting the predicate with the modifier that goes before the predicate. In previous lessons, there have been cases in which a de connects a noun with another noun. That de may be called de$_1$, the de in this lesson is called de$_2$. | zhāng | mea. | (used for paper, table, beds, etc. ) |
| | | | fù | mea. | (used for sets of things) |
| | | | Jiānádā | | Canada |
| | | | yì yuán fù shǐ | | the new year has begun |
| | | | wàn xiàng | | things of various kinds have got new life |
| | | | gēng xīn | | |

## Explanations of the Text

1. The sòng in this lesson means to present (a gift). But the sòng in Lesson Nineteen means to see somebody off.

2. "Wǒ sòng nǐ yì zhāng hèniánkǎ."

   "Wǒ sòng nǐ yì píng Máotái jiǔ."

In this sentence structure there are two elements after the verb. One is a thing and the other is a person. These elements are called double objects.

3. Tòngtong kuàikuài is the doubled up form of the adjective tòngkuai. Monosyllabic adjectives are doubled up in Aa manner. For example: xiāng — xiāngxiāng (de), pàng — pàngpàng (de). Disyllabic adjectives are doubled up in AaBb manner. For example: piàoliang — piàopiao liàngliàng (de), tòngkuai — tòngtong kuàikuài (de).

The doubling up implies a deepening in degree. The last one or sometimes two syllables (the second a and b) of the doubled up adjective should be toneless; sometimes, an er sound is added to these two syllables.

## Sentence Patterns

1.

| Wǒ | | | | píng jiǔ. |
| Nǐ | | nǐ | | zhāng hèniánkǎ. |
| Tā | sòng | tā | yì | tào zhìfú. |
| Mǎlì | | wǒ | (yí) | dǐng jiěfàng mào. |
| Tāngmǔ | | Tāngmǔ | | zhāng dìtú. |
| | | Mǎlì | | zhī māo. |

2.

Zhè { fù duìlián / ge zì (charater) / jù (sentence) huà } shì shénme yìsi ?

## Exercises

1. Read aloud the following syllables:

   gōngxǐ      hèniánkǎ      piàoliang      fēicháng

   kāishǐ      wǎnhuì      shēngmìng      dào qí

   yì yuán fù shǐ      wàn xiàng gēng xīn

2. Tone drills:

   yì zhāng      yì píng      yí gè      yí wèi

hǎo hǎohao（de）　　xiāng xiāngxiang（de）

piàoliang　　piàopiaoliàngliàng（de）

tòngkuai tòngtongkuàikuài（de）

3．Tone and sound discrimination：

gōngxǐ　　—　　kōngxí　　（air-raid）

fēicháng　　—　　féicháng　　（ large　　sausage

casings）

kāishǐ　　—　　gāisǐ　　（wretched）

kèren　　—　　gèrén　　（individual）

wǎnhuì　　—　　wǎnhuí　　（retrieve）

4．Dictation of new words in this lesson：

hèniánkǎ　　shēngmìng　　wǎnhuì　　xīn

piàoliang　　tòngkuai　　yìsi　　nián

tóngxué　　dàjiā　　kāishǐ　　bāo

dōngxi　　kèren　　xiāng　　niàn

5．Substitution drills：

（1）　Hèniánkǎ

Tāngmǔ de yīfu

Mǎlì　　｝ zhēn piàoliang！

……

（2）　Máotái jiǔ

Jiǎozi

Kǎoyā　　｝ hǎo xiāng a！

Kāfēi

……

（3）　Mǎlì

Xiǎo Wáng

Wáng xiānsheng｝ hǎo ｛ piàoliang / cōngming / shòu / dà ｝ a！

Zhōngguó

……

6．Fill in the blanks with either de₁ or de₂：

（1）xīn ＿＿＿＿ yì nián

（2）cōngming ＿＿＿＿ háizi

（3）piàoliang ＿＿＿＿ gūniang

（4）gāoxìng ＿＿＿＿ shuō

（5）tòngkuai ＿＿＿＿ wánr

（6）fēicháng ＿＿＿＿ hǎochī

130

( 7 ) nǔlì ＿＿＿＿ xuéxí

( 8 ) yúkuài ＿＿＿＿ tiàowǔ

7. Translate the following sentences into Chinese：

( 1 ) Mary , Tom and Xiao Wang are having the New Year meal together .

( 2 ) Both Mary and Tom have presented Xiao Wang a gift .

( 3 ) Mary's gift is a greeting card .

( 4 ) Tom's gift is a bottle of Maotai .

( 5 ) The three of them make dumplings together .

( 6 ) They are having a party in high spirits .

# Lesson Twenty-two

**Text**

Xiǎo Wáng：Zhè shì Jiānádà tóngxué Bǐdé.

This is our fellow student from Canada--Peter.

Bǐdé： Wǒ jiào Bǐdé Wēi'ěrxùn. Zhù dàjiā Chūnjié hǎo!

My name is Peter Wilson. Happy New Year to you all!

Tāngmǔ： Wǒ jiào Tāngmǔ.

My name is Tom.

Mǎlì： Wǒ jiào Mǎlì.

My name is Mary.

Tāngmǔ： Nǐ de Zhōngwén hěn hǎo.

You speak Chinese very well.

Bǐdé： Nǎli, hái chà de yuǎn ne.

Well, I've got a long way to go.

Tāngmǔ： Zhēnde, nǐ de fāyīn hěn biāozhǔn.

I mean it. Your pronunciation is perfect.

Bǐdé： Nǐ guòjiǎng le.

You've given me an undeserved compliment.

Xiǎo Wáng：Jiǎozi shú le, dàjiā chángchang.

The dumplings are ready. Please help yourselves.

Tāngmǔ： Wèidào hǎo de hěn.

They're delicious.

Xiǎo Wáng：Méi shénme cài, dàjiā suíbiàn chī diǎn.

The dishes are really inadequate. Please help yourselves.

Bǐdé: Cài bù shǎo, hěn fēngshèng.

There are plenty of dishes.

Xiǎo Wáng: Zhù dàjiā xīnnián xìngfú, gānbēi!

I wish everybody a Happy New Year! Cheers!

Tāngmǔ Zhù nǐ jiànkāng, gānbēi!

Mǎlì: To your health! Cheers!

Bǐdé

Mǎlì: Xiǎo Wáng, biǎoyǎn yí gè jiémùba.

Xiao Wang, give us a performance.

Tāngmǔ: Duì, chàng yì shǒu Zhōngguó gē.

Yes, sing us a Chinese song.

Xiǎo Wáng: Wǒ? Nà hǎo, wǒ xiànchǒu le.

Me? All right. I'll try.

## Vocabulary

| | | | | | | |
|---|---|---|---|---|---|---|
| Zhōngwén | *n.* | Chinese | cháng (chang) | *v.* | to taste |
| xīnnián | *n.* | new year | biǎoyǎn | *v.* | to perform |
| jiémù | *n.* | performance | chàng | *v.* | to sing |
| gē | *n.* | song | xiànchǒu | *v.* | (self-depreciative) |
| biāozhǔn | *a. n.* | standard | | | to make a spectacle |
| shú | *a. v.* | cooked (also | | | of oneself |
| | | pronounced as shóu) | shǒu | *mea.* | (used for songs |
| suíbiàn | *a.* | casual, informal | | | and poetry) |
| shǎo | *a.* | less, few | de | | a word connecting a |
| jiànkāng | *a.* | healthy | | | verb or adjective |
| fāyīn | *v. n.* | to pronounce; | | | with their compli- |
| | | pronunciation | | | ment. It is pro- |
| guòjiǎng | | you flatter me | | | nounced $de_3$. |

## Explanations of Text

1. About complement

Zánmen zhǔnbèi ＜yí xià＞.

Kèren dào ＜qí＞ le ma?

Zánmen chī ＜wán＞ wǎnfàn ＜kāi wǎnhuì＞.

133

Wèidao hǎo ＜jí＞ le.

Wèidao hǎo de ＜hěn＞.

（Wǒ de Zhōngwén）hái chà de ＜yuǎn＞ ne.

In the foregoing sentences the elements in angle brackets are complements. They are used after verbs or adjectives to provide additional information on the quantity and result of verbs and the degree of adjectives. In some cases（as in the last two sentences above）, the structure word de（$de_3$）is used to connect complements with verbs and adjectives.

2. The structure word de

There are three types of de. $De_1$ connects nouns with their modifiers; $de_2$ connects verbs and adjectives with their modifiers; $de_3$ connects verbs and adjectives with complements. The three des are identical in pronunciation: all are toneless; but their written forms are totally different: $de_1$ —— 的; $de_2$ —— 地; $de_3$ —— 得.

## Sentence Patterns

1.
Zhù
$\begin{cases} \text{dàjiā} \\ \text{nǐ(nín)} \\ \text{Mǎlì} \\ \text{Zhāng lǎoshī} \end{cases}$
$\begin{cases} \text{Chūnjié hǎo!} \\ \text{Xīnnián yúkuài!} \\ \text{shēntǐ jiànkāng!} \\ \text{quán jiā (jiātíng)xìngfú!} \end{cases}$

2.
$\begin{cases} \text{Shēntǐ hǎo} \\ \text{Wèidao hǎo} \\ \text{Jiǔ xiāng} \\ \text{Fāyīn biāozhǔn} \\ \text{(Tā)piàoliang} \\ \text{......} \end{cases}$ jí le.

## Exercises

1. Read aloud the following syllables :

tóngxué    Zhōngwén    fāyīn    biāozhǔn

guòjiǎng    suíbiàn    xīnnián    jiànkāng

biǎoyǎn    xiànchǒu    chī diǎnr    chàng gēr

2. Tone drills :

nǎli    biāozhǔn    Xiǎo    Wáng    xiànchǒu

jiǎozi    zhēnde    chángchang    shénme

yì shǒu gē    yí jiàn lǐwù    yí gè jiémù

fāyīn bù hǎo    wèidao bú cuò

3. Tone discrimination :

cháng - chàng              nǎli - nàli

dàjiā - dǎjià ( to fight )    yǎnjing ( eye ) - yǎnjìng ( spectacles )

biāomíng - biǎomíng        biāoyǔ - biǎoyǔ

4. Dictation of the new words in this lesson :

Zhōngwén    xīnnián    jiémù        gē

biāozhǔn    suíbiàn    jiànkāng    shú

fāyīn        guòjiǎng    biǎoyǎn    shǎo

xiànchǒu    chángchang chàng    shǒu

5. Fill in the blanks with de₁ , de₂ and de₃ :

（1）Xiǎo Wáng _____ tóngxué

（2）Shānběn _____ fāyīn ( hěn biāozhǔn )

（3）suíbiàn _____ chī yì diǎnr

（4）gāoxìng _____ chàng gē

（5）chī _____ hěn duō

（6）wèidao hǎo _____ hěn

（7）Xiǎo Wáng cōngming _____ hěn

（8）Fāyīn biāozhǔn _____ hěn

6. Dialogue :

（1）Xiàng Zhāng lǎoshī zhùhè ( congratulate ) shēngri ( birthday ) :

（ i ）_____ .

（ ii ）_____ .

（2）Xiàng Wáng xiānsheng zhùhè Shèngdànjié ( Christmas ) :

（ i ）_____ .

（ ii ）_____ .

（3）If someone says to you :

Nǐ de Yīngyǔ hěn hǎo .

According to Chinese custom , you'd better say :

_____ .

（4）If someone says to you :

Nǐ shì yí gè hǎo xuésheng ( student ) .

According to Chinese custom , you'd better say :

_____ .

7. Learn to sing a Chinese song : *The Shepherdess* ( *In a Faraway Place* ).

# Summary (lessons 20-22)

## Communicative Expressions

1. Asking about days and dates:

Láojià
Qǐngwèn }, jīntiān(shì) { jǐ hào?
                              xīngqī jǐ?

| Month | Days of the Week | Dates |
|---|---|---|
| 1 yuè | xīngqī 1 | 1 yuè 2 hào (rì day) |
| 2 yuè | xīngqī 2 | 5 yuè 22 hào (rì) |
| 3 yuè | xīngqī 3 | 9 yuè 9 hào (rì) |
| 4 yuè | xīngqī 4 | 11 yuè 25 hào (rì) |
| 5 yuè | xīngqī 5 | 12 yuè 4 hào (rì) |
| 6 yuè | xīngqī 6 | qiántiān |
| 7 yuè | xīngqī tiān (rì) | zuótiān |
| 8 yuè | | jīntiān |
| 9 yuè | | míngtiān |
| 10 yuè | | hòutiān |
| 11 yuè | | qiánnián (the year before last) |
| 12 yuè | | qùnián (last year) |
| | | jīnnián |
| | | míngnián (next year) |
| | | hòunián (the year after next) |

2. Expressions of modesty:

The Chinese people strongly believe that modesty is a great virtue. They never feel satisfied with what they have achieved and believe one must not overrate oneself, for he or she has to work harder in order to do better.

So when praised or complimented, they often say:

Nǎli, hái chà de yuǎn ne.

Nín guòjiǎng le!

Even when they have prepared a lot of food for their guests, they still say:

Méi shénme cài.

Zhǐshì (only) jiācháng fàn cài.

This is to show their friends that his or her hospitality has not been fully expressed and they would like their guests to understand and forgive them.

Before giving a performance for friends, they also try to show their modesty:

Wǒ bú huì biǎoyǎn.

Wǒ xiànchǒu le.

## Grammar

1. Different ways of combining words:

Words are combined according to certain rules of relationship. They form various word groups. The following are a few most basic and commonly used combinations:

(1) Coordinative

Wǒ hé nǐ    lǎoshī hé tóngxué

yòu dāng bàba yòu dāng mā

(2) Modifier-modified

xīn de yì nián    cōngming de háizi

tòngtongkuàikuài de wánr

(3) Verb-object

hē kāfēi    chī jiǎozi

kàn diànshì    xuéxí Hànyǔ

(4) Verb or adjective-complement

jièshào yíxià    hǎo jí le

chà de yuǎn    hǎo de hěn

(5) Subject-predicate

wèidao hǎo    Mǎlì piàoliang

wǒ guǎn    tā jiǎnféi

2. The structure of the simple sentence:

(1) Sentences can be constructed by combining words according to the relationships mentioned above. The following is a formula of a simple sentence with all the possible elements arranged in appropriate syntactic order:

(attribute)subject〔adverbial〕predicate＜complement＞(attribute)object

For example:

(Sì gè) péngyou〔gāogāoxìngxìng de〕chī＜wán le＞(yì zhī)kǎoyā.

(Four friends happily had a roast duck.)

(2) You must not think that all these elements are absolutely necessary for any simple sentence in Chinese. This is because, in reality, the structure of Chinese sentences is more flexible than in many other languages. Any word group or even a word, if placed in an appropriate language context and given certain mood and tone,

will become a sentence. For example:

(i) (Shuí shì Měiguó rén?)

　　—Mǎlì hé Tāngmǔ.

(ii) (Nǐ qù nǎr?)

　　—Qù jiàoshì.

(iii)(Shuí qù guo Běijīng?)

　　—Wǒ.

## Understanding China

Major Festivals in China

| Name of the festival | Description |
| --- | --- |
| Yuándàn | *New Year, January 1.* One day holiday. |
| Chūnjié | *Spring Festival.* The 1st day of the 1st moon of the lunar calendar. It often occurs in February. Spring Festival is the most important traditional holiday in China. |
| Guójì láodòng fùnǚ jié | *International Women's Day, March 8.* Working women have a half-day holiday. |
| Guójì láodòng jié | *International Labour Day, May 1.* A full day holiday. |
| Duānwǔ jié | *Duanwu Festival.* The 5th day of the 5th moon of the lunar calendar. People hold dragon boat races and eat zòngzi (glutinous rice wrapped in bamboo leaves) on this day. |
| Guójì értóng jié | *International Children's Day, June 1.* School children have one day holiday. |
| Zhōngguó gòngchǎndǎng chénglì jìniànrì | *Commemoration Day of the Founding of the Communist Party of China, July 1.* On this day in 1921, the CPC was founded in Shanghai. |
| Zhōngguó rénmín jiěfàngjūn jiànjūn jié | *Commemoration Day of the Founding of the People's Liberation Army (PLA), August 1.* The PLA was founded in 1927. |
| Zhōngqiū jié | *Mid-autumn Festival.* The 15th day of the 8th moon of the lunar calendar. It is a traditional festival during which people watch the full moon and eat moon cakes. |
| Jiàoshī jié | *Teachers' Day, September 10.* This holiday was introduced in 1985. |

| Zhōnghuá rénmín gònghéguó guóqìng jié | *National Day of the People's Republic of China, October 1.* This is a two-day holiday. The People's Republic of China was founded in 1949. |
| Lǎorén jié | *Old People's Day.* The 9th day of the 9th moon of the lunar calendar. It was originally called Chongyang Festival. As a custom, people go on outings to ascend a height in order to enjoy a distant view. It was officially declared Old People's Day in 1989. |

## Humour

1. Yànyǔ (proverbs)

Proverbs are set phrases or sentences that spread far and wide among the people in China. They often employ refined and vivid language to reflect profound and important truths. Here you will be introduced to two sets of them. More proverbs will be included in future lessons.

(1) Yì nián zhī jì (plan, key, strategem) zàiyú (to depend on) chūn (spring).

The planning of the year's work begins with spring.

Yí rì zhī jì zàiyú chén(morning).

The planning of the day's work begins with morning.

Yì jiā zhī jì zàiyú hé.

The key to family life is harmony.

Yì shēn (body) zhī jì zàiyú qín (diligence).

The key to a successful career is diligence.

(2) Sì hǎi (sea) zhī nèi (inside) jiē (each and every) xiōngdì (brother).

All people within the four seas are brothers.

Wǔ hú (lake) sì hǎi jiē xiōngdì.

All people within the five lakes and four seas are brothers.

2. Xué Hànyǔ nán (hard) ma?

△: Xué Hànyǔ nán ma?

○: Kāishǐ nán, hòumian (later)jiù róngyì (easy) le.

△:Nà wǒ jiù xué hòumian de ba.

3. Zánmen de

Xīnniáng (bride): Jīnhòu(in future) bùxǔ (not allowed) shuō wǒ de, dōu yào gǎichéng (change into) zánmen de.

Xīnláng (bridegroom): Hǎo de.

Xīnniáng: Nǐ xiànzài gànmá qù?

Xīnláng: Wǒ qù guā (to shave) zánmen de húzi (moustache).

## Introduction to Chinese Characters

The structure of Chinese characters is of two categories: (a) independent structure; (b) synthetic structure. Characters of independent structure are composed of only one part. They mainly include pictographs or characters made up of a pictograph and a symbol. There are not many characters in this first category. Once you have grasped the figural meaning indicated by such characters you will find it very easy to learn them by heart.

Characters of synthetic structure are composed of two or more parts: some are made up of several pictographs while others include a meaning symbol and a sound symbol. A large number of characters belong to this category, and their structures are complicated. However, many of these characters often share a common component, according to which we can divide characters into different groups. Characters of the same group are not only similar in form but also in meaning. This way of grouping characters help us understand them and commit them to memory.

For example, 氵 is a component shared by many characters. It stands for water. Accordingly, all the characters that have the component 氵 are in a way related to water or other liquid. For example:

河(氵 氵 氵 氵 汇 汇 河 河) hé: Huánghé, Hénnán, Héběi, héliú(river);

海(氵 氵 汇 海 海 海 海) hǎi: sì hǎi, hǎiliàng, Shànghǎi, hǎiyáng(sea and ocean);

汉(氵 汉) hàn(the name of a river, from which the Han nationality derived its name): Hànyǔ, Hànzì, Hànzú (Han nationality);

酒(氵 汇 沂 酒 酒 酒 酒) jiǔ: píjiǔ, Máotái jiǔ, pútao jiǔ, jiǔxí (banquet).

Many characters share the radical 女. It was originally written 𡚸, resembling a kneeling woman. Characters that have this part are often related to femininity. For example:

姓(𡿨 女 女 女 奵 奵 姓 姓) xìng: 姓 means to be born of a woman, showing that surname originated in matriarchal society: guìxìng, xìngmíng(name);

好(奵 好 好) hǎo: hǎochī, hǎowánr, hǎoxiàng, hǎoduō(many).

There are also mā, tā(she), jiě, mèi, qī (wife), gūniang(girl), xífù(daughter-in-law), nǎinai (grandmother)….

Other commonly used radicals include:

艹（ 屮屮 ）stands for grass. For example：cài 菜 (vegetable)，chá 茶 tea，huā 花 (flower)，fāng 芳 (fragrance)；

木（ 朩 ）stands for tree and plant. For example：běn 本 (book)，bēi 杯 (cup)，yǐzi 椅子 (chair)，sēnlín 森林 (forest)；

言（ 言 ）simplified as 讠，stands for language or speech. For example：qǐng 请 (to invite)，xiè 谢 (to thank)，shuōhuà 说话 (to speak)，rènshi 认识 (to know)，yǔyán 语言 (language)；

口（ 口 ）stands for mouth or other activities of the mouth. For example：chī 吃 (eat)，hē 喝 (to drink)，chàng 唱 (to sing)，ma 吗，ba 吧，wèi 味 (taste)，tǔ 吐 (spit)；

亻（ 人 ）stands for people, their body and behaviour. For example：nǐ 你 (you)，tāmen 他们 (they)，xiū 休 (rest)，tǐ 体 (body)；

心（ 忄 ）stands for heart, often used to indicate people's feeling or mental activities. For example：nín 您 (you)，gǎn 感 (feeling)，xiǎng 想 (to think)，gǎnxiǎng 感想 (to feel).

责任编辑：周奎杰　郁　苓
封面设计：李士伋
插　　图：李士伋

外国人学中国语

1

北京外国语大学《外国人学中国语》编委会

*

©华语教学出版社

华语教学出版社出版

（中国北京百万庄大街 24 号）

邮政编码 100037

电话: 010-68995871

传真: 010-68326333

电子信箱: 网址: www. sinolingua. com. cn

电子信箱: hyjx@sinolingua. com. cn

北京外文印刷厂印刷

中国国际图书贸易总公司海外发行

（中国北京车公庄西路 35 号）

北京邮政信箱第 399 号　邮政编码 100044

新华书店国内发行

1993 年（16 开）第一版

2006 年第六次印刷

（汉英）

ISBN 7 - 80052 - 309 - 8 / H · 304(外)

9 - CE - 2813PA

定价：33.50 元